needs assessment:

a focus for curriculum development

by

Fenwick W. English
Superintendent of Schools
Hastings-on-Hudson, New York

Roger A. Kaufman
Professor of Psychology and Human Behavior
United States International University
San Diego, California

Foreword by
Delmo Della-Dora

Association for Supervision and Curriculum Development
1701 K Street, N.W., Suite 1100, Washington, D. C. 20006

Price: $4.00

Stock Number: 611-75048

Library of Congress Catalog Card Number: 75-16109
ISBN 0-87120-069-4

Acknowledgments

*Final editing of the manuscript and publication of this booklet were the
responsibility of Robert R. Leeper, Associate Director and Editor, ASCD publi-
cations. Technical production was handled by Maureen Montgomery, Nancy
Olson, Elsa Angell, and Teola T. Jones, with Caroline Grills as production
manager.*

Contents

PART III.
The Curriculum Development Cycle Using a Needs Assessment Base 49

PART IV.
Critical Questions About the Needs Assessment Process **55**

Glossary of Terms with Needs Assessment **64**

Foreword

I found this booklet by Fenwick English and Roger Kaufman to be both interesting and provocative. One need not share their obvious enthusiasm for this particular approach to curriculum development and accountability in order to appreciate the lively and interesting description of their proposals.

The major virtue of what they suggest is a means for establishing controls over curriculum development at the local level, whether it be a school district or an individual school.

The criterion to which I can subscribe wholeheartedly is one which they state as follows, "In order for needs assessment to be valid and useful, it should include the educational partners of learners, educators, and community members. . . ." I would have wished for more attention to have been given to the ways in which *learners* actively participate in the needs assessment process. However the reader who wishes to do this can infer ways in which it might be done based on what the authors have written.

English and Kaufman have produced a useful addition to the growing literature on accountability, curriculum development, and establishment of educational goals which should be of interest to many ASCD members and others as well.

DELMO DELLA-DORA, *President, 1975-76*
Association for Supervision and
Curriculum Development

Introduction

If there weren't any learners, there would not be any curriculum. Curriculum is a valued process for bringing about required and desired changes in learner skills, knowledges, and attitudes so that students can survive and contribute in the world of further schooling and the world of work, family, and interpersonal relationships.

For years curriculum designers have had to rely on insight, expert judgment, and the whims of administrators and community members for their curriculum objectives and design. This procedure has been successful, but only partially. All of us know that our curriculum *could* be better, and now it *can* be better. We now can also further humanize the learning process, for curriculum can at last take into account the unique values and characteristics of the individual learner. The tool for this is *needs assessment,* a process for identifying and defining valid curriculum and instructional and management objectives. This process depends upon a partnership between learners, teachers, and community members. It is flexible and responsive.

The authors have applied this process in several educational situations, and are here attempting to pass along to readers some of the more useful and germane results for those who want to make curriculum more responsive and responsible in the schools.

Fenwick W. English
Roger A. Kaufman

PART I

Background

Rationale

Curriculum is a means to an end. It is the conscious and deliberate shaping of the major elements at the disposal of the educator to reach validated student objectives. These elements represent assumptions about time, space, learning and teaching, and the relationships between teachers and students brought together within varying types of schedules to reach those objectives of which the curriculum stands as the composite configuration. As such the curriculum is the final process tool to be used to reach such objectives and it is subject to a complex set of assumptions and decisions.

In the past curriculum development has been hampered by various assumptions, some of which demand reexamination. Curriculum has not been universally perceived as a means. To some it is the beginning place and the end. The process of curriculum development has been used by them to generate educational goals and objectives. National curriculum projects in the physical and biological sciences and recently in the social sciences have been utilized to develop educational objectives and to specify teaching strategies to reach the objectives within prepackaged units and learner kits.

The resulting confusion with the evaluation of a new curriculum developed in such a manner means that no curriculum can be evaluated against another since both may have competing objectives and approaches. The debate about curriculum degenerates to a battle over educational philosophies. Another result is the hodgepodge of curricular packages which now exist in the schools, particularly in the secondary curriculum. The reforms of the past decade have led to intensive curriculum development in some fields, presumably those which relate to national defense, and little attention to others less immediate or deemed less critical to national survival.

Arguments about philosophy still permeate the curriculum field. The topics of humanization and individualization are sometimes approached as separate "curricula" unto themselves and discussed as general "good things" toward which curricula and schools must be shaped. It is still unclear which types of curricula promote or detract from humanization or which are amenable to individualization, or whether individualization is clearly inappropriate for some educational objectives based upon the principle of sharing group experiences. While much talk has been spent on defining multidisciplinary approaches, curricular inquiry and curriculum building have focused on the disciplines as singular entities despite the best intentions of the scholars. Implemented in the school, very few national curricula have served as a function actively to reorganize the school, confront the isolation of departments, or create more sensitive staffing patterns or learning environments.

Curriculum development has tended to increase rather than diminish the isolation of learning and the learner within separate areas of the school and has reinforced the current concepts of singular disciplines. The selection and adoption of curriculum at the local level have advanced on the basis of developing compatibility within a certain philosophical perspective, or have advanced on the basis of the availability of relatively sophisticated curricular support systems in the way of teacher and student workbooks and other supplementary materials. A local Board of Education still has precious little data upon which to decide on the merits of a particular curriculum compared to others or to the status quo (which is often left undefined).

Personnel at the local level are still very much the prey of national standardized tests by which the effectiveness of the newly adopted curricula must be judged. One reason that school people seem to have been "captured" by the standardized test makers is the lack of specificity of ends. In the absence of well defined objectives for school systems and individual learners, standardized tests seem to offer a readily available substitute. Despite the protestations of teachers and administrators in local school systems, without valid system output objectives, standardized tests appear to offer an "easy out." And while some educators bemoan being judged by such tests, they seem to lack the will or knowledge to create a viable substitute. In the absence of local goals and objectives which have been developed and validated, the precision and certainty of the standardized test loom very much as the placebo assumed (incorrectly) to have no negative effects.

More recently, criterion-referenced test items and test instruments have been developed and are being developed in order to supply some test items which relate directly to critical (or those judged critical) skills, knowledges, and attitudes directly and specifically rather than the more general norm-referenced, or standardized tests. Thus, instead of testing in domains of knowledge, the criterion-referenced tests measure specific behaviors.

But that does not seem to be enough. Measurability is not the same as validity—just because we can measure something does not mean that the item is correct or even necessary. This, therefore, is a major flaw in the measurable behavioral objectives movement when measurable objectives alone are the referent for beginning of curriculum design—there should be some positive and documented referent for the validity of the objective. This referent can be supplied by a formal set of tools and procedures called *needs assessment*.

What Is Needs Assessment?

Needs assessment is a process of defining the desired end (or outcome, product, or result) of a given sequence of curriculum development. As such it is a "curriculumless" process, that is, it is neither a curriculum itself, nor should it embrace any set of assumptions or specifications about the type of curriculum which ought to be developed to best reach the ends desired and defined.

Needs assessment is a process of making specific, in some intelligible manner, what schooling should be about and how it can be assessed. Needs assessment is not by itself a curricular innovation, it is a method for determining if innovation is necessary and/or desirable.

Needs assessment is an empirical process for defining the outcomes of education, and as such it is then a set of criteria by which curricula may be developed and compared. Which curriculum, that is, which configuration of people, time, and space produces the types of outcomes desired?

Needs assessment is a process for determining the validity of behavioral objectives and if standardized tests and/or criterion-referenced tests are appropriate and under what conditions.

Needs assessment is a logical problem solving tool by which a variety of means may be selected and related to each other in the development of curriculum.

Needs assessment is a tool which formally harvests the gaps between current results (or outcomes, products) and required or desired results, places these gaps in priority order, and selects those gaps (needs) of the highest priority for action, usually through the implementation of a new or existing curriculum or management process. In order for a needs assessment to be valid and useful, it should include the educational partners of learners, educators, and community members in the process for defining gaps (needs). It should also include an external referent for gap determination, such as economic survival in the operational world to which the learner goes after legally exiting from our educational agencies.

Accountability

Much of the debate about accountability muddies the difference between means and ends in education. To some educators, at the point at which specific ends can be related to dollar costs, the school system becomes "accountable." Thus, the installation of such a tool as PPBS, with its own derivation of educational program objectives, often determines the "essence" of accountability. However, without a method or means to determine the validity of the objectives outside of programs, all that may have been created is a device to indicate how ineffective current programs are in terms of dollars. Until and unless the validity of the program objectives and the programs themselves are challenged, PPBS offers very little in the promise of educational improvement. Likewise other managerial techniques such as MBO (*Management by Objectives*) or systems analysis offer little in the promise of educational reform, neither do they assist in the validation of practice compared to validated objectives. These technologies streamline the means, and yet the ends often remain vague and undefined, and the technologies themselves cannot be fairly assessed except for their ability to generate more sophisticated data for administrators. They seem bent on offering increased reliability while largely ignoring validity.

Much of the debate concerning accountability appears to center on the premise that everything is not measurable. The argument goes that since everything which may be a legitimate objective of schooling is not measurable, all that accountability offers is a means to assess the trivial. If everything that is important cannot be measured, then, so goes this type of logic, nothing should be measured. There is a certain smugness about this stance until one realizes that many schools now concentrate unduly upon the trivial; tests assess the ability to regurgitate information; and our institutions systematically dehumanize large groups of students by making them believe they are inferior or stupid in a variety of ways. Sensible accountability is not the perfection of means; rather it is first the delineation and validation of ends, and then a systematic comparison of means (processes or techniques) defined to reach the ends. The process of needs assessment should precede any implementation of PPBS, MBO, system analysis, systems analysis, writing behavioral objectives for teachers or students, or curriculum development.

The move toward accountability has been characterized by some as an attempt by those most concerned with economy to impose industrial cost accounting methods upon an essentially non-industrial based enterprise. Yet the argument against even the cost accounting movement ignores the current "factory model" of education which is preeminent within our educational system: students are grouped on chronological age, teachers sorted by the age of the students and by curricular disciplines, and learning equated with time served and defined as sets of equal exposures to information presented.[1] The current system runs well without diagnosis and without individualization. Attempts to introduce more flexibility in terms of curricula, scheduling, and grouping have run aground time and time again because the system of mass education is a non-performance, time-based assembly line model of schooling. At the worst, accountability, if it is defined incorrectly as PPBS or MBO, merely tells us which combinations of interactions and inputs prior to schooling appear to make some assembly line models and variations more effective on standardized tests.

To talk about humanizing this system is so much more than making teachers more "sensitive" to youngsters or than organizing an alternative school or introducing more inductive methods in the sciences. Rather it is the fundamental analysis of our basic day-to-day operational assumptions and a direct challenge to our definitions of administrative control of education. Humanization discussed in isolation from this model, or for that matter accountability however defined, proceeds through a logical set of arguments, perhaps devoid of the process for defining the ends of education, and then selecting the means most promising to assist educators in reaching the "promised land." For this reason we object to labeling the process of needs assessment as de facto accountability or dehumanization. The latter are only means to ends which a proper, sensitive, and responsible needs assessment defines.

Accountability is a process of demonstrating that the organization has accomplished that which it said it would accomplish.[2] Accountability for "means" (such as team teaching or differentiated staffing, or

---

[1] A factory type analogy to the schools was used by Alvin Toffler in *Future Shock.* New York: Random House, Inc., 1970.

[2] See: L. M. Lessinger, D. Parnell, and R. Kaufman. *Accountability: Policies and Procedures.* New London, Connecticut: Croft Educational Services, 1971.

even needs assessment and system planning) alone is a deception which might result in efficiency without effectiveness. Accountability, to be useful and humanistic, should be a process relating to demonstrating the achievement of results—results which have been demonstrated and documented to be valid, useful, humane, appropriate, and timely. It is our contention that a formal needs assessment will allow for a useful, humanistic accountability. And while we are at it, why should we not be accountable for humanism?

Critical Assumptions of Needs Assessment

Like any other process, there are certain assumptions behind engaging in a useful needs assessment. No process in education can be "value free," for even professing no value is in itself a value. The following assumptions appear to undergird a needs assessment.[3]

1. *Reality can be known, understood, and represented in symbolic form.*

The process of needs assessment is firmly rooted in empiricism. In order to undertake such an assessment what is currently undefined (unknown) must become known and accurately defined. What comes to be known can be represented (and manipulated) in some sort of symbolic form such as words and numbers. While reality is infinite, it can be represented and divided between knowns and unknowns. Definite parameters can be developed to represent what is known, and the unknown can be represented as well. Since reality is never static and the boundaries of the knowable are expanding, unless this assumption is part of the needs assessment, a false picture may be provided of the known. The elasticity of the framework of the known is reinforced by the concept of feedback which in reality is the expansion of what is knowable.

2. *Reality is not static: assessment must be a continuing process.*

The expansion of what is knowable assumes reality is never static, that is, it moves as the sum total of man's knowledge increases, and some procedure inherent in needs assessment must incorporate this assumption. The feedback loop or the constant reevaluating of the ends of education to determine shifts in priorities responds to a fluid reality.

[3] There are a number of extant models for needs assessment, most of which we feel are more accurately termed "solutions assessment." In this report we are defining a product or outcome oriented model only.

3. *Perceptual fields can and should be changed relative to the ends of education.*

It has been observed by the philosopher Eric Hoffer that man does not first see and then construct categories to see, he or she first constructs categories and then he or she sees. From the beginning of man's look into life and the universe he or she gropes for meaning within constructs he or she makes to extract meaning from those observations. Even as a scientist looks for patterns in observing natural phenomena, the criteria for determining what to look for and how those observations are coded are the product of a priori categories and assumptions. Needs assessment can be a process for determining the validity of the categories by which people observe the universe.

4. *Everything can be measured.*

On some scale of measurement, everything in education can be measured. There are four scales of measurement in psychological terms: nominal, ordinal, ratio, and interval.[4] While it is not possible to measure such human emotions as love, or inclinations such as creativity or curiosity on a ratio or interval measurement scale, it may be possible to assess them on the cruder indices at the nominal or ordinal level. Often the blockage to a discussion of educational objectives is not whether they are desirable but whether they can be measured.[5] By allowing for a discussion of measurement to include an honest and somewhat less reliable form of measurement to be developed on a nominal or ordinal basis, the discussion can be moved to a true consideration of the desirable ends of education.

5. *The aims or outcomes of education can be made specific.*

The considerable experience with behavioral objectives has built up a repository of skills within the profession about making educational aims specific. Although the type of taxonomy utilized for such purposes may be different, it is possible to make "operational" the aims of education by breaking global and vague outcomes into smaller, more assessable pieces. One of the excuses for not being specific about the aims of education comes from the argument that since our schools serve a pluralistic society, to make the outcomes of schooling explicit would be to seriously impair the effectiveness of the schools

[4] For a more in-depth review of this presentation see: Roger A. Kaufman. *Educational System Planning.* Englewood Cliffs, New Jersey: Prentice-Hall, Inc., 1972.

[5] For the characteristics of measurable classroom instructional objectives see: Norman E. Gronlund. *Stating Behavioral Objectives for Classroom Instruction.* New York: Macmillan Publishing Co., Inc., 1970.

because there are inherent value conflicts within the larger society that are not reconcilable. Only if the actual outcomes of the schools remain vague can the schools function. This is a serious indictment of today's education if one pauses to analyze the implications of this position. Studies such as those by Jencks[6] and previously the Coleman Report[7] have revealed the extent to which the schools actually discriminate against various subcultures in the nation. The mythology of the schools' serving a pluralistic society has been explored by a number of more modern writers.[8] Minority subcultures are particularly sensitive to the inequalities inherent within current definitions of schooling.

Most previous work in determining if there is a consensus about the problems and functions of education shows a remarkable agreement about what the schools are doing and not doing.[9] The Gallup Polls published by the Kettering Foundation[10] have served to indicate that the public, as it represents the viewpoints of many publics in supporting the schools, is in more agreement than some educators would like to admit. These preliminary documents show that not only are there commonly delineated goals for education in the nation, but that irrespective of subculture, the desires and aspirations of those subcultures to capitalize upon the school as the institution to attain the "good life" are remarkably uniform.

6. *The recipients and supporters of the schools should be involved in determining their goals and effectiveness.*

The hegemony of the professional in solely deciding what ought to go on in the schools has been severely cramped as state after state has moved toward implementing some form of accountability legisla-

---

[6] Discrimination by reinforcing factors found in the larger environment. See: Christopher Jencks et al. *Inequality: A Reassessment of the Effect of Family and Schooling in America*. New York: Basic Books, Inc., Publishers, 1972.

[7] The Coleman Study illustrated that traditional variables within the school such as the size of libraries, modernity of facilities, etc., did not affect pupil achievement. See: James Coleman. *Equality of Educational Opportunity*. Washington, D.C.: United States Office of Education, 1966.

[8] Colin Greer. *The Great School Legend*. New York: Basic Books, Inc., Publishers, 1972.

[9] See: *The Reform of Secondary Education*. A Report of the National Commission on the Reform of Secondary Education. Charles F. Kettering Foundation. New York: McGraw-Hill Book Company, 1973. The goals were derived from those of the 37 states and then used by George Gallup in a public opinion poll.

[10] See: *The Gallup Polls of Attitudes Toward Education, 1969-1973*. Bloomington, Indiana: Phi Delta Kappa, 1969-1973.

tion.[11] In some states, citizen participation has been mandated at the local school level where members of the community become actively involved in assessing the effectiveness of the schools. Salisbury has explored what he calls "the myth of the unitary community."[12] It is from the assumption that the community is essentially homogeneous that the professional can lay claim to being the sole guardian of a singular institution serving the public. The moment that various sub-cultures begin to assert their desire to become actively involved in shaping the schools, the hegemony of the professional is challenged.

Persons in education must face the fact that in no public institution can the professionals afford to become the sole managers of that institution. There is no guarantee that if solely in charge of public education, educators would not allow their own demands for security and domination to usurp goals and objectives that may challenge the viability of the institution as it has come to be defined by those professionals. For any institution to remain responsive it cannot afford to be "captured" by any one group, particularly by those who operate it on a day-to-day basis. It is in the best interest of the public and the professional educator to develop a shared responsibility for the functioning of the schools in our society.

7. *There is a relationship between organizational specificity and productivity.*

There is a great deal of human energy and conflict in school systems.[13] Much of the conflict exists as a result of the lack of clarity in the purposes of the schools. As the ends of the educational process are vague and undefined, it is difficult to know where to begin improving schools except to make such statements as "we should try harder."[14] If students are not learning, what can be done? One of the first strategies should be to define what it is students should be learning. There can be little basic improvement in the managerial practices of school systems until such systems define their objectives

[11] For a complete review of state accountability goals write to the Cooperative Accountability Project of Denver, Colorado, State Department of Education.

[12] Robert H. Salisbury. "Schools and Politics in the Big City." *Harvard Educational Review* 37(3): 408-24; Summer 1967.

[13] For a review of the assumptions about conflict in the schools and the unproductive ways it is viewed see: Fenwick W. English. *School Organization and Management.* Worthington, Ohio: Charles A. Jones Publishing Company, 1975. pp. 3-8.

[14] The lack of specificity of ends can also lead to an impossible situation in evaluating educational innovations. See: John Pincus. "Incentives for Innovation in the Public Schools." *Review of Educational Research* 44(1): 113-44; Winter 1974.

in assessable terms.[15] It is due to the lack of such specificity that the public ends up having to reconcile scores on standardized tests with their tax bills. Now that the nation has entered a period of pupil enrollment decline, the public finds it even harder to understand, with fewer pupils to educate, why their bills and the test scores are not better able to coincide.

The lack of specificity in education protects no one and it can lead to all kinds of quackery in the schools. Old ideas in new names, peddlers of schemes for this and that find a great receptiveness in the hallways of schools, legislatures, and Congress. There is a feeling expressed by some state legislators that the schools cannot be improved except by radical means with ideas that may be contrary to good education. Yet the lack of specificity within the schools provides no criteria for an intelligent decision about means and ends. Laymen express great exasperation with educators with warm hearts but fuzzy intentions, who resort to slogans as answers to the confounding problems of the schools in our times. It is assumed that specificity of ends will lead to specificity and responsiveness of means.

8. *Productivity and humanization are compatible as dual outcomes of improved schools.*

Productivity is viewed with great skepticism by some educators who feel that it inevitably means that those practices which are the least expensive will come to be protected and enshrined as the ultimate criteria of productivity. Let us define productivity as the ability to solve problems in the most effective and efficient manner available.

There is evidence that the public will pay high taxes and bills for those areas in which the outcomes are tangible. Witness the growing and acceptable costs of providing educational programs for the child with learning disabilities, and the costs of programs in vocational-technical or career education which appear to have gathered a successful political lobby at most state levels and at the national level as well. An undifferentiated set of goals and objectives which ignores the individual differences of our school clientele forces students into an unspecified mass and deprives educators of the base upon which to indicate that straight dollars on a per pupil basis are not enough to meet the needs of the students.

There is no reason to believe that, as the bulk of the students are differentiated even more, the public will not become more, rather

---

[15] This is basic to humanizing schools. See: "Shaping Schools into Purposive Humanistic Systems," Chapter six. *School Organization and Management, op. cit.,* pp. 176-99.

than less, responsive to sincere attempts to apply more dollars to educate students. The fear that the public will insist upon dollar criteria is only justified as the schools fail to become more responsive to a greater range of human diversity than the system will admit. More money to reinforce present practice may not be justified. More money for improved practice, improved diagnosis toward identifiable and specific ends, can create a greater willingness to fund the costs of public education. If humanization is defined as the encapsulation of practices which recognize and act upon a greater range of pupil diversity and purpose to bring about individual growth and achievement while maintaining diversity, then productivity and humanization are linked to specificity of outcomes.

Summary

Needs assessment is a tool at the disposal of the educational curriculum developers enabling them to look at the problems of the schools once again. It is a process for assisting in the discrimination between means and ends, between the purpose of the schools and the curriculum as the total configuration of the elements used by the professional to arrive at validated ends. Curriculum is a tool to define and outline the steps to become responsive, accountable, and productive.[16] Curriculum can only be assessed in view of what it was shaped to accomplish.[17]

[16] See: Fenwick W. English, James K. Zaharis, and Roger A. Kaufman. "Educational Success Planning: Reducing Chance as an Aspect of School Innovation." *Audiovisual Instruction* 16(5): 20-22; May 1971.

[17] Roger A. Kaufman. "The Concept of Needs Assessment—Back to Basics." *Texas School Board Journal* 20(4): 10-12; June 1974.

PART II

How the Curriculum Developer Does a Needs Assessment

The steps to a needs assessment revolve around a simple model. A need is a gap, or a discrepancy between two indices, that is, a future desired condition and the status quo. The concept of "need" defined as a gap was first used by Ralph Tyler in his historic work on the development of curriculum at the University of Chicago in the early fifties. Tyler wrote:

> Studies of the learner suggest educational objectives only when the information about the learner is compared with some desirable standards, some conception of acceptable norms, so that the difference between the present condition of the learner and the acceptable norm can be identified. This difference or gap is what is generally referred to as a need.[18]

Earlier definitions for "need" included gaps in processes, while the later work of Kaufman and Corrigan emphasized the concept as relating only to gaps in results or outcomes.[19] The concept of needs assessment was developed into a longer process of system analysis in the late sixties in *Operation PEP* (Preparation of Educational Planners) in California.[20, 21]

---

[18] Ralph W. Tyler. "Basic Principles of Curriculum and Instruction." Syllabus for Education 305. Chicago: University of Chicago Press, 1950. pp. 5-6.

[19] Roger A. Kaufman, Robert E. Corrigan, and Donald W. Johnson. "Towards Educational Responsiveness to Society's Needs, A Tentative Utility Model." *Journal of Socio-Economic Planning Science*, 3: 151-57; August 1969; and Kaufman, *Educational System Planning, op. cit.*

[20] Roger A. Kaufman. "A System Approach to Education: Derivation and Definition." *AV Communication Review* 16(4): 415-25; Winter 1968.

[21] Roger A. Kaufman. "A Possible Integrative Model for the Systematic and Measurable Improvement of Education." *American Psychologist* 26(3): 250-56; March 1971.

In order to perform an outcome or "discrepancy analysis" it is necessary to have measurable statements about future desired conditions and then to assess the present in terms of its distance from those desired conditions. The future desired conditions are educational goals or objectives stated in terms of desired and validated pupil learning behaviors. How these behaviors come to be defined and validated and later set into comparative assessments of what is currently resulting in the school system is the focus of this section.

The Generic Steps of Needs Assessment

The generic steps of needs assessment[22] are as follows:

1. Planning to plan: charting means and ends;
2. Goal derivation;
3. Goal validation;
4. Goal prioritization;
5. Goal translation;
    5.1 The development of performance indicators;
    5.2 The development of detailed performance objectives;
6. Validation of performance objectives;
7. Goal re-prioritization;
8. Futuristic input to goal ranking;
9. Rerank goals;
10. Select testing instruments or evaluative strategies for assessing the current state;
11. Collate data gathered;
12. Develop initial gap or "need statements";
13. Prioritize gap statements according to step 4;
14. Publish list of gap statements.

There is also a set of post needs assessment steps which "act" upon the data produced in the needs assessment. These are:

1. Interpolate gaps by program and level;
2. Conduct diagnostic/planning sessions to develop implementation strategies to meet identified needs;
3. Budget for implementation strategies;
4. Fund strategies;
5. Implement strategies;

[22] For a review of some of these steps see: Raymond G. Melton. "Needs Assessment: Common Sense in Education." *Catalyst for Change* 4(1): 9-11; Fall 1974.

6. Reassess gaps via feedback;
7. Repeat steps of needs assessment process.

Planning To Plan

Even if there were sophisticated manpower available to undertake a needs assessment, it still could not be accomplished overnight. A great deal of planning should precede the needs assessment. Questions about involvement, how the idea will be introduced, anticipating problems, and developing the capacities to handle the data when gathered are only a few of the queries which must be answered.

Most school systems anticipate a time period of approximately six months to two years to complete the full cycle of a needs assessment. The time line will vary depending upon the sophistication of the school system, the personnel to be involved in the assessment, and the staff provided. Another important factor will be the utilization of goals and objectives that the system has already developed. Finally the existence of several years of data accumulated via testing will also be an important consideration in calculating the overall time required. It should be strongly emphasized that a needs assessment should be a continuing activity, not a one-shot affair.

Who Shall Be Involved?

If classical educational planning has suffered greatly from any particular weakness, it has been the lack of meaningful citizen and student input in the process of planning, particularly in the establishment of goals for the school system. In many school systems, the prerogatives of the professional to decide solely upon the type and kind of community involvement have been directly challenged through decentralization or by state legislatures themselves in developing accountability legislation.

The lack of citizen involvement in determining what was desirable and feasible has led to any number of political catastrophes such as the controversies over sex education as a curriculum priority, and more recently the violence and conflict in West Virginia over the selection of school textbooks.[23] No matter how much the professional

[23] In reviewing the recent textbook dilemma in West Virginia, former New Jersey Commissioner of Education Carl Marburger noted, "It seems to me that if parent participation had continued in Kanawha, it is unlikely that the situation would ever have become so aggravated." See: "The West Virginia Textbooks." New York Times, October 24, 1974, P.C. 41.

would like to convince himself or herself that he or she is the best judge of what should be taught in the schools, the professionals do not (contrary to some popular belief) control the schools. Much could be avoided if professionals would not see every plan for citizen involvement as an attempt to erode their power, safety, and authority.

The exclusion of citizen participation in school affairs has been a consistent pattern of at least the past fifty years that is now in the process of a dramatic reversal. The pattern of exclusion is partly a result of distrust of citizen meddling which is greatly feared, by and large, at the school level by teachers and principals. Part of the acrimony over the means of education is a result of the lack of professional leadership in focusing parent and citizen input on the outcomes (ends) of education. That the schools are obviously failing large numbers of students while these same schools are protesting citizen interference in the process of education has aroused a marked response in citizen and legislative ire.

Any question regarding the necessity for citizen and student involvement in establishing a needs assessment for the school system can be referred to the basic tenet that the schools belong to the people. Moreover, such involvement is critical in the needs assessment process because if educators are to make decisions (that is "act upon" the data produced from the process), they will find themselves isolated if there is not a sense of ownership or proprietorship of those decisions by the students and community.

The most severe test of the needs assessment process comes in "acting upon" the needs, or "closing the gaps" identified in the procedure. Such a point comes when the dollar begins to change directions and when a shift of priorities occurs within the school system, each with constituencies in the community. At such a time the result can be politically dangerous if those same constituencies do not "own" the information and if they have not been involved in formulating solutions to the needs (gaps) identified.[24]

The Phenomenon of Finite Resources

Needs or educational gaps are prioritized because while needs are infinite, human resources (dollars, time, people) are finite. This forces a human system to rank its goals, and to meet critical needs first,

[24] For an excellent presentation of sampling techniques of the community see: Appendix B in: John R. Stock and Dionne J. Marx. "Citizens' School Survey: Surveying the Public's Educational Goals." Worthington, Ohio: School Management Institute and the Battelle Memorial Institute, 1971. 18 pp.

thus delaying less important ones. As citizens come to see this in a practical sense at the local level, they may be willing to raise local taxes, or to support a bond issue, or to lend their services to special levies of one form or another. While resources are finite, they are relatively elastic. With more information and a sense of ownership in sifting the priorities of the school systems, educators may come to see that the people are willing to expand the flow of resources to the school system. Thus, the boundaries of resources expand to meet more needs than before. Partially, this is a result of making clear what the priorities of the school system actually are.

Will the Board's Prerogatives Be Usurped?

Additional fears for the role of the Board of Education have been raised about needs assessment. If the Board sees the needs assessment process as a plebiscite of the public they may feel threatened since they may hold views which they believe they have been elected to implement. Therefore the Board's fundamental responsibility for direction setting must not be encroached upon but enhanced via the needs assessment process.[25]

The needs assessment does not curtail any prerogatives of the Board. It is not a plebiscite, it identifies only "gaps" between what is desired in terms of results and current outcomes. The needs assessment identifies the "what," it does not identify the "why," or the "how." The needs assessment process will help the Board continually focus on community concerns, it is not a substitute for Board action or inaction. The Board retains its essential role as a decision-maker, both in evaluating goal priorities suggested by the community, and in recommending action to close identified gaps and meet existing goals.

If, however, the Board has not had its eyes upon the "whole picture," or if individual Board members have been elected on "one issue" platforms, the needs assessment process will help them to focus, even serve as a forcing function formally to identify and examine the needs of the total school system and to prioritize these in relationship to one another. The needs assessment will assist the Board in establishing the "big picture" and a long range view and help them find criteria for

[25] The role of the board in the needs assessment process was explored in: "The Board's Role in Curriculum Development." Speech before the New York State School Boards Association Annual Convention, New York City, October 1974, by Fenwick English. (Mimeographed.) 2 pp.

evaluating the effectiveness of administrative proposals and administrative performance. It is because school boards have not had a method for abandoning the trivia that calls for alternative tools of citizen involvement and input have arisen.[26] Both the role of the general community and the Board's ability to represent its various constituencies can be enormously enhanced via a needs assessment.

The Role of the Teachers Association/Union

A nervous teachers association or union may wonder if the needs assessment will mean another innovation, or will usher in a wave of more trouble with the board or administration. Groundwork with the leaders of the union or association that frankly, candidly, and honestly explains that it is not an innovation, rather a process for determining if innovation is even necessary and a process to foster greater staff participation in determining the priorities of the school system, will pay rich dividends.

[In most school systems, it is the teachers who have a major, if not preeminent role in goal translation and the identification of "gaps" and strategies to deal with the "gaps." Since teachers comprise the largest professional input to the process, their voice will be heavily felt in the formulation of direction and the application of ideas to move the system toward the identified goals.] In the process of developing a workable relationship, all partners will share in the accountability for the results—no longer will the teacher be the "fall guy." [The needs assessment process clearly helps to delineate the shared responsibility for acting upon the gaps once these are identified and located.|

Weighting the Input to the Process

Kaufman believes that the major constituencies involved with a needs assessment should have equal value; he therefore assigns no weighting to any one audience in goal setting.[27] Each constituency is therefore of equal worth. However, in the actual development of the performance indicators, performance objectives or the like, the professional carries the major responsibility for goal translation (as well as for implementation). While it can be argued that community representatives and students could also be involved in these steps, in most

[26] For an example of dealing with the trivia as a pathology of a board see: David Rogers. *110 Livingston Street.* New York: Random House, Inc., 1968.

[27] Kaufman, *Educational System Planning, op. cit.*

cases they have not been. It takes some training to engage in writing performance objectives, a skill some professionals have not yet mastered very well.

Most systems using needs assessment have not gone beyond the initial weighting of the input. Very few even attempt to validate the objectives from the three constituencies proposed by Kaufman and almost universally used in the field: professionals, community, and students. Gaining confidence from the public and students and staff will mean spelling out ahead of time how the data will be treated. It is important, we think, for educational and political reasons, both in the initial assessment and later acting upon the data, that these three basic constituencies be equally weighted.

Dealing with Ambiguity and Anxiety

If the school system proposing needs assessment has been largely functioning at the survival level, living from day-to-day crises, and buffeted by forces of accountability, decentralization, or internal strife, then some explanation of what needs assessment is and is not will be necessary in order to quell some of the rumors which will certainly result in the discussion about doing one. A general rule of thumb is that the more specific the information, the less anxiety, inasmuch as ambiguity leads to speculation and rumor even more than does specificity. In times of declining enrollment when job security may be an issue, it will be important to state ahead of time the intended uses of the data and what kinds of administrative and instructional decisions will be made with the data; also how much influence various groups will have in the input process, the problem identification, the solution derivation, and the implementation and evaluation of the entire process.

The more people know what is happening, why it is happening, and how data will be used, the more considered will be their input. If teachers, parents, or students suspect that needs assessment is merely a "paper exercise" to satisfy some legal requirement, or to soothe professional guilt feelings about making most of the real decisions, they will not take much time to become identified with or become involved with the process itself. If at the end of the needs assessment process, the Board and the administration are proposing various solutions to which the teachers, parents, and students are reacting with indifference or hostility, then there was not enough involvement, not enough explanation, and certainly no feeling of ownership from these groups about the problems or the solutions identified. To avoid being in this dilemma, the Board and administration should take great care in planning carefully and committing themselves to meaningful and substantive involvement. These factors should be incorporated and outlined in the "planning to plan" phase of the needs assessment.

Goal Derivation

To undertake a needs assessment, or outcome gap analysis, it is necessary to have two basic indices: a clear statement of a measurable, desired, and future outcome, and a clear indication of the current results in relation to the desired outcomes. The "gap" between the two is a need or discrepancy.

There are two basic approaches to deriving future desired outcomes. The first is to gather a group together (it can also be done by mail) and have the group list the desired results. Upon agreement, an assessment of what is currently the state then follows. A simple discrepancy list can then be constructed. This is called a compilation of "felt needs," since such lists begin with the concerns (or internal judgments or "feelings") of the group as to what ought to be present (or absent) in any given situation. One of the problems with beginning with "felt needs" is that what ends up being expressed as a "gap" is the absence of a "pet solution" rather than a statement of difference between a given level of pupil learning or growth and a desired level. It is not uncommon to find among lists of "felt needs" examples of the following statements:

"Lack of bilingual program"
"We should be individualizing instruction more"
"Our school must have a flexible schedule"
"We are not accountable here for results."

Bilingual programs, individualized instruction, flexible scheduling, and accountability are means to ends, not ends in themselves. Most "felt needs" lists are enumerations of such solutions rather than a listing of discrepancies between two states of learner growth, that is, desired and actual.

Goal derivation is the conscious process of stepping away from the current program, its current curriculum and methods of implementation, and its biases and assumptions. It requires thinking about desired learner growth needed to survive in a rapidly changing society and the setting down of a list of outcomes or skills, knowledges, and attitudes that students should acquire in order to cope with such a rapidly changing society.[28] After these have been validated, ranked, and changed into detailed performance terms, an assessment is made of current levels of achievement or growth to determine the gaps. As a result of determining that gaps or "needs" do exist, a search is then begun in a diagnostic phase to determine if there is enough individualized instruction, or if rigid schedules prevent good teaching from occurring, or if a budget system could be derived to coincide with determining if the current programs are ineffective and costly for the results obtained. From the gaps come useful clues for tracing down problems with the tools and processes of implementation.

For this reason, we recommend that goal derivation begin away from the level of "felt needs" with concentration upon future desired learner outcomes first, rather than beginning with a "rap session" about what's wrong with the schools. Another approach equally as dangerous as the "felt needs" approach is to begin drafting and defining needs from the current condition via standardized testing and accepting the test results as an indicator of need.[29] For example, some states may accept the results of some standardized test as the indicator that any student two or more grade levels below is in "need" of a special program, or of ESEA Title I funding, or of additional aid. This approach begins with the test, assumes its validity, and defines the target population accordingly, and then leaps to the solution—a tendency anytime one uses the word "need" to describe anything other than an outcome gap! The test may not be valid at all for the goals and objectives of the school system, but if used in this manner it circumvents any local participation and ranking of educational priorities. A test should be selected after the goals and objectives are derived and validated, not before. Tests should be selected to derive a data base compared to local goals and objectives, and not used in the absence of such data to indicate "gaps" in current educational programs.

It is paradoxical that a "needs assessment" derived from standardized tests will, on a large enough sample, always show that 50 percent of the population are below average, and at least 14 percent or more two standard deviations below (or for that matter, above) the mean. Thus, to allow a standardized test to define a "need" is to build in failure from the beginning for at least a percentage of students in the

---

[28] For an example of big city goals see: "Report of the District Goals Review Committee," Los Angeles Unified School District, October 1974. 51 pp.

[29] New York mandates extra state aid for students based upon the results of a standardized achievement test in math and reading. Districts are forced to follow the formula.

school system. The testing base should be selected with care after the goals and objectives have been developed, and the nature of those objectives be used as one criterion for test selection. A school system which allows itself to define needs solely from standardized tests has signed away its prerogatives and local options for program development, and the responsibility for meeting the unique needs of its own clientele and community accordingly. That is not accountability, it is closer to irresponsibility.

A Philosophy of Education: Is One Necessary?

Often one hears about the necessity for developing a philosophy of education and then developing goals and objectives from it. This is to add a step which may not be necessary in needs assessment. Most philosophical statements of education are muddled attempts to define the nature and purpose of schooling and the type of educational program desired by the patrons or the Board. Once in a while some clear statements of desired pupil learning are encountered as well, often jumbled into the same paragraphs that describe the type of school and program desired. Beginning with such a "philosophy" as a base to define future desired conditions leads educators into the same trap as that of beginning with "felt needs." Too often, statements about schools and programs, which are means to ends, are confused with what students ought to be learning in those schools and programs.

Most attempts at writing a "philosophy" represent an attempt to draft something in writing that pleases everyone and offends no one. They have to be sufficiently vague as to boggle a precise interpretation. For example, "Develop each child to his or her own capacity" is loose enough so that one may be a hero or a bum depending upon who is subjectively evaluating the criterion! A philosophy has one other disadvantage; that is, it is impossible to validate in the abstract. If one should encounter a philosophy, how is it determined that it represents the considered opinion of the majority of the patrons, or what does it mean? Some philosophies are distinctly anti-empirical; that is, validation is done by rhetorical and logical argument, not on the basis of human input, perception, and observation. Such statements are "above" validation in the sense that public reaction means very little. While beginning to derive goals of education for students that are subject to some empirical test is not an impossible task from a philosophical statement, it is a step which may be more confusing than helpful.

An empirical philosophy of education is assumed in an approach to needs assessment. Input and reaction from teachers, parents, and students with equal weighting, mean that human perception and human values are a part of an approach to defining the outcomes of education. After the goals are defined and translated into performance or behavioral terms, and then into programs by consensus, it would be far more meaningful to write a philosophy of education as a summary to the future desired conditions, rather than a prerequisite prior to discussing those desired conditions, and probably far more accurate and consistent as well.

Goals represent non-time specific and desired outcomes of the schooling years in terms of pupil behaviors. As such they represent minimum expectancies, not maximum attainments, that is, they represent the establishment of a floor not a ceiling. There is nothing to limit school systems from going beyond the minimum expectancies. Yet the "floor" represents a basic commitment, that is, a promise that unless a student is severely impaired the system will guarantee that he or she would acquire those skills, knowledges, and attitudes prior to graduation. This commitment does not ignore the fact that the school or educators do not control all the variables associated with school progress, but that they do have at their disposal some of the costliest means to deal with society's most precious asset and its stake on the future, that is, the young.

How are goals established? Goals can be developed from groups of educators, citizens, and students who "brainstorm" them. There are also many sources of educational goals. Many states through state departments of education are developing and validating goal statements. One of the first was a special task force in Pennsylvania developed by the Educational Testing Service. Some of these goals were:

1. Quality education should help every child acquire the greatest possible understanding of himself and an appreciation of his worthiness as a member of society;
2. Quality education should help every child acquire understanding and appreciation of persons belonging to social, cultural, and ethnic groups different from his own;
3. Quality education should help every child acquire to the fullest extent possible for him mastery of the basic skills in the use of words and numbers.[30]

[30] Henry S. Dyer and John K. Hemphill. "Highlights of a Report from Educational Testing Service to the State Board of Education of the Commonwealth of Pennsylvania." Princeton, New Jersey: Educational Testing Service, June 30, 1965. 21 pp.

Other state departments have similarly published lists of goals such as:

Florida,

All students shall acquire a knowledge and understanding of the opportunities open to them for preparing for a productive life, and shall develop those skills and abilities which will enable them to take full advantage of those opportunities—including a positive attitude toward work and respect for the diginity of all honorable occupations.[31]

Michigan,

Michigan education must assure the development of youth as citizens who have self-respect, respect for others, and respect for law.[32]

Texas,

All students should achieve knowledge about comparative political systems with emphasis on democratic institutions, the American heritage, and the responsibilities and privileges of citizenship.[33]

Goals may be derived from various types of group activities; however, more and more such derivations are from state sources. A perusal of state lists of goals illustrates a remarkable similarity in basic aims.

Goal Validation

While there are many types of validity, for purposes of a needs assessment validity is established, in part, by consensus among the constituencies identified who are involved in determining whether or not those goals listed shall be used by the system itself. Thus, we are essentially dealing with "face validity," for purposes of constructing an instrument to rank order the goals of the system.[34] Goal validation consisted in one system of mailing to 100 citizens, including professional educators, a survey requesting input as to whether or not the

[31] Department of Education. "Goals for Education in Florida." Tallahassee, Florida: the Department, n.d. 11 pp.

[32] Department of Education. "The Common Goals of Michigan Education." Lansing, Michigan: the Department, September 1971. 11 pp.

[33] Texas Education Agency. "Goals for Public School Education in Texas." Austin, Texas: the Agency, October 1970 2 pp.

[34] Face or content validity is a nonstatistical type of validity. See a discussion of validity in: N. M. Downie and R. W. Heath. *Basic Statistical Methods*. New York: Harper & Row, Publishers, 1965. pp. 222-27.

proposed goals for the school district should be included, excluded, or amended for later ranking or prioritization purposes.[35] The purpose of goal validation is to determine whether or not a set of goals should stand for the minimal scope of the basic commitment of the system to its clients and to the supporters of the system. While the goals may be rearranged almost infinitely, there should not be a goal which is outside of the goal list, that is, it should be inclusive.

Another dimension is necessary in a useful validation procedure in addition to those which are generated by the partners—an external referent and set of criteria which relate to performance outside of the educational system. Kaufman, Corrigan, and Johnson suggest a utility referent of the skills, knowledges, and attitudes necessary to achieve the minimal levels of survival in, and then hopefully contribution to, the world after legally exiting from the educational agency.[36] Thus partner-perceived needs are then compared to an external set of criteria about that which actually is necessary in the world of work, the world of human relations, and the world of values and productivity. It is this addition of criteria external to the partner perceptions ("felt needs") that is a hallmark of a practical and useful needs assessment.[37] If there are differences between the partners and the utility data, a "negotiation" must be completed, usually with a modification in the perceptions of the partners, or occasionally the collection of new empirical data to substantiate or modify the original empirical information. Information concerning external survival and contribution may be gleaned from a number of sources, including census and employment data, Department of Labor figures on consumption and survival, levels of income and productivity, the *World Almanac,* and the like. The importance of this external empirical information cannot be overemphasized, for it provides empirical reality to the perceptions of the educational partners.

Goal Prioritization

The next step upon validation of the goals of the system must be performed in a ranking exercise. There are several ways to accomplish ranking or prioritizing of the goals. Most common is a survey or questionnaire. The State Department of Education in Maryland used the Motor Vehicle Administration's list of persons possessing a driver's

[35] Fenwick W. English. "Report on a Partial Return on County Wide Needs Assessment." Florida: The School Board of Sarasota County, May 9, 1973. (Mimeographed.) 6 pp.

[36] Kaufman, Corrigan, and Johnson, *op. cit.*

[37] Kaufman, *Educational System Planning, op. cit.*

license and mailed out a survey to 23,990 citizens comprising students, professional educators, and school board members. The Department received a 51.5 percent response. The sample ranked the following goals as most important:

1. Mastery of reading skills;
2. Ability to arrive at independent decisions;
3. Development of self-respect;
4. Ability to apply knowledge and skills to the solution of real life problems;
5. Knowledge of the personal and social consequences of critical health problems (such as smoking, drug abuse, alcohol, work hazards);
6. Skills required for employment in their selected occupations by students planning to enter the job market.[38]

Another procedure for goal ranking is the Q-sort technique.[39] This technique enables a person to rank order a number of goal statements. Each goal carries a number to identify it. As the goal is withdrawn from a series of card pockets it is given the value of rank assigned to it by the respondent. For a group it is fairly easy to sum the values given to each of the goals and divide by the total number in the group to compute an arithmetic mean for each goal which is then rank ordered by mean scores to indicate the group's overall priority attached to the goal compared to all the goals.

Often one hears the question, "Why is it necessary to rank the goals? They are *all* important!" The fact of the matter is that goals of education as they are translated now (mostly by default and tradition) are given priorities within school districts. The reading program may be most important, but it may receive less support by the Board than the interscholastic athletic program. When educational goals are ultimately translated into budgetary commitments, administrative decisions must be made as to where dollars must be allocated to attain the most important goals of the system. Unless goals are formally ranked such decisions are often impossible since there exist now political constituencies actively involved in perpetuating current funding levels of some programs. Shifts within a school budget made necessary by more or less constant resources must have as a rationale the criticality of the

[38] Maryland State Department of Education. "Goals and Needs of Maryland Public Education." Baltimore, Maryland: the Department, November 30, 1972. 24 pp.

[39] Fred Kerlinger. "Q Methodology." In: *Foundations of Behavioral Research.* New York: Holt, Rinehart, and Winston, Inc., 1964. pp. 581-602.

purpose of funding commitment. While all goals are important, they are not *equally* important, particularly as a basic commitment to all children as a minimal expectation, or "floor" educational commitment.

Goal Translation

After goals have been ranked, they must be translated into measurable terms, or performance standards (if they are not already in this form). To do this in one step is often too big a jump for the translators. For this reason some needs assessment procedures now include an intermediate step, that is, moving from general, global goal statements to performance indicators. Performance indicators are what they imply, that is, an "indication" or mark of the goal. Generally, goals are so broad as to take many objectives to capture their full scope and intent. An example of performance indicators is taken from the New York State Education Department's pamphlet on "Goals for Elementary, Secondary, and Continuing Education in New York State."

> *Goal:* Mastery of the basic skills of communication and reasoning essential to live a full and productive life.
> 1. Communication skills (for example, reading, writing, speaking, listening, and viewing);
> 2. Computation operations (for example, mathematical conceptualization, problem solving, data collection);
> 3. The logical process of thinking creatively, critically, and constructively in problem solving, planning, evaluation, analysis, research, etc.[40]

Items 1, 2, and 3 above are performance indicators; that is, they begin to bench mark in more specific terms, but not yet in full performance statements, what is meant in the goal, "mastery of the basic skills of communication and reasoning." Often the question is asked, "How many objectives should be written to capture an educational goal, that is, when does one stop writing objectives?" The answer is fairly easy with the utilization of performance indicators. After a brainstorming session with staff and others who agree that a full range of indicators appears to meet the full intent of a goal, a performance objective is drafted to further define each performance indicator. The performance indicator provides one more level of specificity of the school district via a process of successive approximation. Successive

[40] New York State Education Department. "Goals for Elementary, Secondary, and Continuing Education in New York State." Albany: the Department, February 1974. 20 pp.

approximation refers to the process of becoming increasingly, by steps, more specific, beginning with global goals and deriving specific performance objectives. Reality is approximated and approached, never fully captured.

Another example of deriving performance indicators is supplied by Idella Moss.

> *Goal:* The student will acquire and develop a concern for moral, ethical, and spiritual values and for the application of such values to life situations.
>
> *Cognitive Indicators:*
> 1. Perceives the purpose and function of moral, ethical, and spiritual values;
> 2. Perceives criteria by which moral, ethical, and spiritual values are tested or judged;
> 3. Perceives processes/procedures by which moral, ethical, and spiritual values may be modified or changed.
>
> *Affective Indicators:*
> 1. Is aware of moral, ethical, and spiritual values;
> 2. Accepts responsibility for his role as a participant in representative situations that require application of moral, ethical, and spiritual values;
> 3. Associates personal consequences of responses in representative situations that require application of moral, ethical, and spiritual values;
> 4. Declares commitment for appropriate responses in representative situations that require application of moral, ethical, and spiritual values;
> 5. Habitually responds appropriately in unstructured or spontaneous situations that require application of moral, ethical, and spiritual values;
> 6. Consistently chooses appropriate responses in structured or contrived situations that require application of moral, ethical, and spiritual values.[41]

Moss has stated that when teachers and other professional staff members begin the process of translating goals into performance statements, an excellent "forcing function" is to use the two taxonomies of educational objectives.[42, 43] Another approach would be simply to draft

---

[41] Idella J. Moss. "Working papers of the Sarasota Needs Assessment." Sarasota, Florida, 1974. (Xeroxed.) 12 pp.

[42] Benjamin Bloom et al. *Taxonomy of Educational Objectives: Handbook I: Cognitive Domain.* New York: David McKay Company, Inc., 1956.

[43] David Krathwohl et al. *Taxonomy of Educational Objectives: Handbook II: Affective Domain.* New York: David McKay Company, Inc., 1964.

objectives for each performance indicator and then cluster them into the various types of objectives. The advantage to the forcing of objective development into the categories is that it has a tendency to broaden the scope of the objectives so that a more realistic array of objectives is developed. If the scope appears to be too narrow, additional performance indicators can be developed.

The Development of Performance Objectives

Much has been written in recent years regarding the process of developing educational performance objectives.[44] The idea behind developing an objective is to make it time specific, indicate clearly the required behaviors including attitudes expected of the learner, and the conditions by which those behaviors will be judged to be acceptable after the curriculum or intervention has been implemented.[45]

Once sets of performance indicators have been developed for each of the ranked and validated educational goals, objectives can be developed, sometimes more than one for each performance indicator.

Moss developed a simple format for translation of performance indicators. (See Diagram #1.) The educational goal is clearly a complex one, far beyond some of the simple educational goals which state a required mastery of reading at some percentile level of a standardized test.

For the goal involving skills and habits involved in critical and constructive thinking, the following may serve as indicators of that goal.

1. The student is able to use criteria (such as relevance, causation, and sequence) to discern a pattern, order, or arrangement of ideas, concepts, or materials in a document or a situation.

2. The student will be able to recognize the organizational principles or patterns on which an entire document or work is based.

3. The student is able to arrange and combine elements or parts so as to form a whole:
   a. to produce a unique communication;
   b. to produce a plan or proposed set of operations;
   c. to derive a set of abstract relations.

---

[44] For an excellent overview of the abuses of behavioral objectives see: Arthur W. Combs. *Educational Accountability: Beyond Behavioral Objectives.* Washington, D.C.: Association for Supervision and Curriculum Development, 1972.

[45] Robert Mager. *Preparing Instructional Objectives.* Palo Alto, California: Fearon Publishers, Inc., 1961.

4. The student will be able to produce a set of explanations to account for given phenomena by:
   a. creating a classification scheme;
   b. creating an explanatory model;
   c. creating a conceptual scheme;
   d. creating a theory—to account for a range of phenomena, data, and observation.

Using the *Taxonomies of Educational Objectives* as a tool of translation, a list of ten educational goals may require 150 educational objectives. These objectives are stated for the terminal or exit point for the school system, that is, for a school district with a high school, the objectives are stated for grade twelve; for a K-8 system, eighth grade. The objectives are minimal expectations, or behaviors which all students will acquire in some acceptable way within the time spent in the school system providing that they are not impaired in some way from learning them.

Sometimes it is asked, "Why begin at the end of the educational sequence, why not at the beginning?" Once again the objectives have been derived from educational goals which are statements of future desired conditions (learning) which should occur somewhere within the educational system. Just as it is not wise to begin with "felt needs" because they are too often confused with current school system behavior and/or existing techniques, so it is unwise to begin developing fourth grade goals without knowing what the fifth grade, eighth grade, or twelfth grade goals are and how these in turn relate to survival and contribution in the external world. The selection of goals by grade level or by some other method for establishing evaluation points within the organization must begin with the "floor" expectations at the end of the educational sequence. This does not inhibit the school system from providing more to the student, but it does serve as impetus to examine the school program, scheduling, funding, and staffing so as to ensure that students will acquire the basic expectations prior to the time they are permitted to graduate.

Subgoals for the school system are extrapolated from the terminal goals and broken into simpler parts, skills, knowledges, and attitudes by interpolation from the last expected or global goal for the system. That is, if such and such learner behavior is required here, then what are the subskills, knowledges, and attitudes which will be required before, and at what general levels would they appropriately be placed? Findings from the social sciences as to types of learner psychological

Goal: The student will acquire and use the skills and habits involved in critical and constructive thinking.

Performance Indicator: The student is able to apply principles and generalizations to new problems and situations.

Step 1
State the conditions under which behaviors may be observed (specify most meaningful type of evaluation).

Example for above:
A contrived classroom construct or simulation, either on paper or developed within small groups which may be observed by the teacher.

Step 2
State the institutional expectancy (percent of grade group of which behavior is expected or the degree of individual mastery desired).

Example for above:
After the contrived situation passes, the learner is able to specify verbally or on paper the following:
1. The processes by which the group set criteria which were then instructive and/or appropriate in deriving generalizations appropriate to problem solving by the group;
2. The limits within which a particular group generalization or principle tested the limits of the group solution(s);
3. The type of decision reached by the group and whether or not the decision was supported by the group's generalizations and logic.

Step 3
State the required proficiency in the performance of the behavior.

Example for above:
The learner will exhibit verbally or by listing on paper the major strategies selected by the group and those which led to a conclusion warranted by that strategy.

Step 4
State the evaluative instrument or technique to be used.

Example for above:
The learner will indicate in an accompanying essay or written explanation as judged by the teacher his ability to infer particular qualities or characteristics not directly stated from clues available in the situation. He will give the assumptions upon which the group functioned and by which certain solutions were then generated.
5. The student perceives extrapolation behavior as facilitating his comprehension of a given problem or situation.
6. The student willingly specifies or requests limits within which a particular principle or generalization is true or relevant in seeking to solve problems or understand a given situation.
7. The student consistently justifies or requests justifications of particular courses of action or decisions in a new situation by the use of appropriate principles or generalizations.

Diagram #1. Format for the Translation of Performance Indicators into Performance Objectives. Developed by Idella Moss.

readiness and evidence of ability to solve problems can be brought to bear to ascertain approximate points in the school system at which mastery should occur. The approach is something like a child learning to walk. Most children learn to walk somewhere between nine months and two years. If a child does not walk within that time period suspicion is raised about the possibility that something may be physically or psychologically impairing the child from walking. Preventive action may be taken in the form of medical or psychological diagnosis and/or treatment.

It seems to us that requiring all children to learn some skill or acquire some knowledge or attitude at a fixed point in the school system ignores all that is known about learning in human beings. Rather such learning should be stated as expected to occur within certain time or developmental spans, so that in reality the learning expected to be mastered upon exit from the system would have only not been mastered by a fractional part of the school population at that time, and so that preventive measures would have been taken very much earlier in the system when certain students were not learning the subskills necessary for terminal skill or knowledge mastery.[46] This would require the development of a support sub-system, and system flexibility which does not exist in most school systems. It implies a fundamental change in the operation of most schools and school systems, that is, movement away from a time-based definition of learning to one which is growth-based and responsive to learner need. Most school systems do not use educational feedback (knowledge of results) because it is not currently required for the system to function. Once schools must assume responsibility for learning, they must move away from a time-oriented definition of learning and become responsible for learning per se as measurable changes in skills, knowledges, and attitudes.

Validation of Performance Objectives

As any critic of performance objectives can easily substantiate, almost anything can be translated into performance terms, that is, learner behaviors. The process of establishing a performance or behavioral objective is not a process to establish its validity, except to

---

[46] The concept of "terminal objective" has been disputed in a precise translation which may mean learning ceases. The concept of "parameter objective" has also been used. See: Joseph M. Conte and Fenwick W. English. "A Theoretical Construct for Mediating Instruction in the Social Sciences." *Audiovisual Instruction* 13(3): 249-53; March 1968.

say it is either a performance objective or it is not. Whether or not the objective should be applied to the schools is another matter.

We are not at the point in the development within the needs assessment process where a list of performance objectives has been produced to match sets of performance indicators derived from educational goals. Only the educational goals have been validated and ranked. Are the performance objectives representative of the goals? This is essentially a question of validity regarding content. And content validity has two dimensions within the process. The first is a matter of determining the accuracy of the translation from goal to performance indicator to performance objective. The second is a matter of scope. While it may be determined that the performance objectives for a given educational goal do in fact represent what the critical audiences meant when they ranked it by assigning a value to it, all the objectives which may capture the full intent of the goal may not be present. Thus, while the objectives represent an accurate translation, they are not all the objectives which are required.

The exit performance objectives must then be validated, again by the three basic groups involved in validating the educational goals: parents and community, students, and professional staff. Such groups must be asked, "Is this what you meant when you ranked this first?" and "Are all the objectives below representative of what you meant when you ranked this goal as important?" There are a number of ways to do this. If the total number of goals is not too long, then a telephone survey could suffice.[47] If they are too long to recall in this format they could constitute the basis for a door-to-door sampling of the community with a trained group of parent or student volunteers. Finally, a paper questionnaire or survey form could be used. At this point, stratified random samples could be designed from the students, teaching staff, and community. What the system requires is feedback about the educational objectives in relationship to the educational goals. One more feature could be added within this step, that is, asking the respondent to rerank the educational goals now that he sees what they look like translated into more specific statements. Again validation consists of having each respondent group approve at a previously determined level of acceptance that the objectives represent the intent and scope of any given educational goal.

[47] A telephone survey was used by the State Education Department in New York to sample administrators at random on educational goals. See: Robert E. Lamitie. "Summary of Elementary, Secondary, and Continuing Education in New York State Goals Telephone Survey Report." Albany: State Education Department, January 15, 1975. 3 pp.

Educational Goal Re-prioritization

Some educators involved with needs assessment have found it necessary to build into the process several points for reconsideration of the primacy of some educational goals. For example, Moss found in Florida that when teachers examined the affective counterparts to some of the educational goals, they saw that they would assign different ranks to them based upon the translation. Also as the affective objectives began to unfold, varying commonalities undergirding a number of cognitive objectives were discovered. This tended to elevate the importance of the affective dimensions of the educational objectives and created a second list of educational goals which may be parts of goals from the original list of ranked educational goals.

For a school system which wants to have a second list of ranked goals, once performance indicators and objectives have been developed, a second sampling of students, staff, and community may be accomplished. This may form the base for a second validation of the educational goals themselves. Actually any one of the steps in the needs assessment process may be repeated and fed back into the previous steps to perform the feedback function. This is one of the ways that needs assessment should be self-correcting and take into consideration shifts in educational goal priorities over time, since no list of educational goals ranked once would ever maintain the same importance over time, particularly if any of the "gaps" or "needs" had been met successfully by the school system.

Futuristic Input to Goal Ranking

One of the basic pragmatic questions facing the curriculum developer is that of immediacy. Needs assessment as outlined thus far actually represents a systematic culling of perceptions of a number of identified constituencies. None of these constituencies has a monopoly on future developments, that is, it is assumed none has a crystal ball. A source such as Toffler's *Future Shock* indicates the tremendous movement already underway which if projected into the future portends enormous changes in living and the quality of life in the nation and the world. To what extent would the educational goals ranked by the citizenry, educators, and students reflect these changes? Would the culling of current perceptions merely result in an endorsement and perpetuation of the status quo?

Depending upon the breadth of the input in the various groups ranking educational goals, there may be some danger that the school system would become shaped by a studied moment at our place in time. Of course, the feedback loop and the repeating of the needs assessment steps at selected intervals in the future provide one check against becoming locked in on a transitory set of needs. The second is to build into the process some studied and considered attempt to analyze the future and use this as a data base upon which to rank or rerank educational goals.

The Delphi Process developed by Helmer[48] of the Rand Corporation is one such procedure. The Rand Corporation has developed a more or less standard set of futuristic goal statements[49] for such use, though the use of the indices in education must be viewed as not very widespread at this time.[50] Basically, the Delphi Procedure is a tiered sequence of eliciting probability statements about future occurrences in the world in any given area, from foreign missile capabilities to medical advancements. It is possible to develop sets of educational goals based upon probable conditions which may be regnant in the world at some agreed upon point in the future.[51]

The curriculum developer may desire to use the Delphi Technique as a method for generating educational goals, validating educational goals, or reranking educational goals. While there are some drawbacks to the use of a procedure like the Delphi, nonetheless it does provide a systematic method for attempting to balance the development of educational goals between present and future, and can serve as one more input to establishing the educational priorities of various goals.

Also useful in "calibrating" the future for inclusion in the needs assessment procedure and resulting data and objectives are studies relating to the future world culture. One such effort, showing possible future trends, was reported by Harman.[52] This work, which emanated from the Stanford Research Institute, also indicates future directions. Inclusion of future-oriented objectives is critical if we are not to repli-

---

[48] Olaf Helmer. "Analysis of the Future: The Delphi Method." Santa Monica, California: The Rand Corporation, March 1967, P-3558. (Xeroxed.) 11 pp.

[49] This list is used in one study. See: W. T. Weaver. "An Exploration into the Relationship Between Conceptual Level and Forecasting Future Events." Unpublished doctoral dissertation, Syracuse University, 1969. 347 pp.

[50] For a good source of futuristic data see: "Education Now for Tomorrow's World." Report of the Curriculum Committee of the California Association of Secondary School Administrators, 1970-2000. Burlingame, California, 1968. 80 pp.

[51] James S. Waldron. "The Delphi Process: Some Assumptions and Some Realities." Paper prepared for presentation at the 1971 Annual Meeting of the American Educational Research Association. (Xeroxed.) 17 pp.

[52] Willis W. Harman. "Nature of Our Changing Society: Implications for Schools." In: Philip K. Piele *et al. Social and Technological Change: Implications for Education.* Eugene, Oregon: ERIC/Center for the Advanced Study of Educational Administration, 1970. pp. 1-63.

cate yesterday's education (and results) now and in the future—we cannot afford to "freeze" in time and ignore the future. In spite of the fact that predictions are tenuous indeed, they are better than assuming that no predictions at all can be made, and not preparing learners for tomorrow. If nothing else, learners can be prepared to identify as well as solve problems as part of the objectives and curriculum, and thus be able constantly and consistently to change their own skills, knowledges, and attitudes as they live the future and cope with it.

Rerank Goals

Based upon research and predictive studies such as the Delphi or some other futuristic input data, the goals may be reranked by the participants or as a result of the input from a group which has studied the future and made recommendations to that effect. This step is the concluding one in formulating the first index to perform a needs assessment. A needs assessment is the process of formulating gaps or discrepancies between two sets of criteria, a list of future desired conditions and results, and a list of current, existing (not necessarily desired) conditions and results. All of the steps so far are those involved with creating a future, validated, and desired set of conditions for learners. In reality the school system is establishing a set of output indicators for itself in terms of learner growth. These can become the indicators of assessment for the system and its various programs, not of how much the latter cost.

The Concept of "Out-of-Discipline" Educational Goals

While it is possible to perform a needs assessment within a particular discipline (history, art, industrial arts, etc.) and a skill area (reading, typing, etc.), this is not recommended as an initial step. Educational goals are rarely confined to one discipline, the origin of which may be the result of historical accident rather than of considered theoretical development.

One of the strongest points of a needs assessment for the curriculum developer is that the resulting "gaps" can serve as a useful and powerful impetus for reexamining the way the curriculum has been divided in schools. If "gaps" are shown to exist in the communication skills, perhaps such communication should be viewed outside of speech, journalism, drama, or English, and serve to remind the curriculum developer that such skills are an integral aspect of all of those school "subjects." If, however, a needs assessment were permitted to be undertaken only in English, with no attention to journalism, drama, speech, or even survival in the "real world," then the resulting "gaps" could only be a reinforcer to the English program. If one of the reasons that there are "gaps" in the achievement of students is the method in which the curriculum is traditionally defined, then the power of the needs assessment to call this into question will be lost. If "gaps" are located in English, they may come to be acted upon in English. For this reason educational goals must be "curriculumless" in the sense that they are "outside" of the school curriculum.

One good method for assisting the curriculum developer in viewing educational goals outside of the curricular disciplines is by examining the goals in light of "survival skills." Such a tack was taken in Oregon in formulating a basic set of educational goals.[53] This approach also prevents a lot of in-house bickering over the "importance" of the various disciplines in the school. To avoid endless and fruitless debate over whether mathematics or science, social science or English contains the most primary goals, goals are considered outside of these curricular delineations. Later they may be located back within disciplines as a matter of determining budgetary priorities and implications of acting upon revealed "gaps" in the performance of students within the school system.

Upon the conclusion of the steps described, the curriculum will have a detailed set of performance objectives which have been validated and ranked and represent a measurable set of conditions or directions toward which the school system moves in a deliberate fashion. The next series of steps is aimed at determining how well the system is currently reaching those desired conditions.

The Selection of Testing Instruments/Developing a Data Base for Gap Determination

The selection of various testing instruments should be a deliberate matter of determining how current levels of student performance are in comparison to desired levels of such performance. The desired levels of student performance are defined first. Previously we had commented upon the practice of defining desired levels of performance from existing levels of performance, that is, by beginning with standardized tests as an assessment of current levels and by using the gaps between those current levels as desired levels.

There are a number of built-in problems with this latter approach,

[53] State of Oregon, Department of Education. "Oregon Graduation Requirements." Section I, II, III, and IV. Salem, Oregon: the Department, September 1973.

not the least of which is the usurpation of the professional staff, citizens, and students in predetermining what should be of most importance in the school program and curriculum prior to any testing being initiated. The second is that the determination of "gaps" becomes what the test can measure or assess per se and not any consideration of what it cannot measure and whether that is not more important than what is being measured.[54] Much of the "flack" about accountability stems from using tests alone as the chief determiner of program or school system adequacy. A needs assessment which is solely defined in terms of standardized test data may be totally inaccurate and may lead a school system to overstress the unimportant in the name of that which can be measured.

Testing instruments ought to be selected with an eye as to validated educational objectives broken down by skill or performance levels in the schools from the terminal, or exit behaviors desired. These behaviors have been defined not as fixed points, but as "bands" within which student growth is assessed over a period of time. It is unrealistic to believe that at any fixed point in time all the students would be exactly at that point in their developmental or learning process. Objectives must take into consideration these differences in achievement.

If one of the educational objectives is that, "Upon graduation a student will be able to read a given editorial from the *New York Times* placed into the format of a reading test at the 85 percent comprehension level and be able to identify specific passages of editorial bias,"[55] then the assessment or testing strategy would be to cut out several pages from the paper and administer them to graduating seniors. Another approach might be to select some standardized reading test which has the same level of reading difficulty as the paper and assume that the ability to read at the same level of the paper on the test would stand for an assessment of the ability to read the paper per se. The latter type of rationale is common in education when direct assessment is difficult or objectives are unclear as to what they really mean.

Likewise assessment at lower points in the school system could reflect the mastery of the designated subskills, knowledges, or attitudes, established at whatever points have been designed to gather such data in the school system. The curriculum developer will be most

[54] See: Stephen P. Klein. "The Uses and Limitations of Standardized Tests in Meeting the Demands for Accountability." *Newsletter of the Center for the Study of Evaluation*, UCLA 2(4): 1-12; January 1971.

[55] This objective would be measurable on a nominal or ordinal scale as stated, and is therefore a "goal" as used by Kaufman in his educational outcome taxonomy. See: Kaufman, *Educational System Planning, op. cit.*

confounded with assessment in the affective area. The same set of conditions prevail. Are there currently instruments upon which acceptable scores could be interpreted as indicative of a learned attitude, or will such attitudes have to be directly assessed via observation? In the affective areas our measurement scales are considerably more crude and certainly less reliable.[56] In some cases schools or a school system may have to develop its own attitude inventories or scales with expert assistance. In other cases, anecdotal data may have to suffice as indicators of attitudes toward school, or to facets of school programs or subjects.[57]

In other ways, many of the educational objectives will relate to attitudes and knowledges necessary for later lifetime activities. In such cases evaluation of school programs may have to be similarly delayed to permit "downstream" assessment to take place in the form of graduate followup studies based upon utilization of key skills learned in the schools. Also, the school will have to devise simulated activities to assess whether or not, given a set of circumstances, learners will use the desired skills. A good example is a first aid course. The principles of first aid may be tested on a paper and pencil test. Learners may practice giving mouth-to-mouth resuscitation on dummies, but the real test may come many years later. Interim assessment occurs in school. The actual assessment may come later. Meanwhile, many "in lieu" situations will have to be created to approximate ways of assessing cognitive, affective, and psychomotor growth.

The selection of instruments should be a careful one and should proceed under the supervision of those most qualified to know the limitations, strengths, and weaknesses of the tests. Some eye to data collation and what kinds of decisions may ensue after the data are gathered should also be anticipated. Rather than abandon an objective because there is no test available, a school system should move toward gathering data which may be representative of an attitude or skill. The lack of a ready-made test or assessment instrument should not change the fundamental importance of an objective after it has been validated and ranked. It should be used to spur the curriculum developer to establish as reliable and valid procedures as possible to gather the data required to indicate how well the students have mastered the objective itself.

[56] See: Walcott H. Beatty, editor. *Improving Educational Assessment: An Inventory of Measures of Affective Behavior.* Washington, D.C.: Association for Supervision and Curriculum Development, 1969. 164 pp.

[57] See: Eugene J. Webb *et al. Unobtrusive Measures: Nonreactive Research in the Social Sciences.* Chicago: Rand McNally & Company, 1973.

Data Collation

Once the various instruments and procedures for data gathering have been implemented to gather information about current levels of student performance, the data collected and available, it will have to be collated into appropriate tables, graphs, charts, and other summative and descriptive materials.[58] A myriad of considerations must be given to data collation. First, who is the consumer of the material? Is it the Board, the professional staff, the community, the students? Perhaps the most detailed information should be provided to those by whom decisions must ultimately be made about what to do with the "gaps" as the primary consideration. The educational consumer (students and parents) should be given a forthright accounting of current levels of performance with as much additional information as may help to establish the reliability and validity of the instruments used. A frank disclosure of the lower reliability of attitude scales will be necessary. The state of the art does not enable us to be too precise about some things; this is not an indication of their importance, but perhaps an indication of their complexity. We are convinced that citizens understand this much better than educators believe they do.

Develop Initial Gap or "Need" Statements

At the point at which the curriculum developer can make statements about the gaps in learner performance, between what is desired and the actual performance in measurable terms, the statement regarding that difference is a "need." A list of prioritized and clustered gaps constitutes the needs assessment. What has been done up to this point is the creation of measurable yardsticks for the assessment to occur.

Need statements are listed without reference as to the cause or reason. They are simple statements of fact, that is, the difference between what was expected and what actually occurred. These are some examples:

1. Fifteen percent of the senior class could not read an editorial from the *New York Times* with at least 80 percent comprehension as measured by a criterion-referenced instrument prepared by the teacher and approved by the department chairman.

[58] See: "Simplified Educational Assessment: A Manual of Nontechnical School Evaluation Techniques." Albany, New York: State Education Department, October 1974. 62 pp.

2. When given a description of a situation listing faulty conclusions, 23 percent of the ninth grade students could not identify the line of reasoning which produced at least ⅓ of the faulty conclusions on a multiple choice test.

3. Two of three third graders could not identify the process by which certain numerals were associated with the operation of addition when asked to respond verbally by their teachers in various types of classroom situations.

4. Eighty-six percent of the fifth grade students did not perceive themselves as participants in quantitative situations that required a knowledge of numbers, symbols used to represent numbers, or any system by which certain of the symbols could be combined as measured by simulated situations prepared by their teachers and rated by them on a matrix listing various types of responses possible.

5. Two percent of the first graders at Hillside School, after a field trip to the zoo, could not find some way to express what they had seen through a picture, story, poem, or by being provided an "opportunity to act out" how various animals looked as determined by the records of the teacher of which mode of response children decided to select 2-3 days after the trip.

6. After being shown a film, "The Evolution of Law and Human Society," 11 percent of the eighth grade pupils would not make any commitment to any situation that demonstrated a need for the application of law as a process for a democratic government to survive as measured by their verbal responses taped by their teachers.

7. After a walk through the surrounding woods, only 6 percent of the first grade students could not recall at least three sounds they had heard or imitate them, draw a picture of the source of the sounds, or explain the source of the sound as peculiar to the woods as measured by a check list kept by the teacher.

The above "need" statements occurred at various points in the school system. In reality some of the elementary grade expectations represent clusters of more complex skills at the upper and secondary grades which have been broken into subobjectives on the basis of grade level. They could just as well be broken into continua and stated in relationship to individual students instead of on the basis of grade levels. For example: Two-thirds of the ten-to-twelve year olds tested were able to explain verbally or in writing the relationship between heat (a source of energy) and steam or by drawing a picture which illustrated how steam is produced with heat as approved by the curriculum supervisor.

Often it is feared that such objectives are the epitome of convergent thinking. They do not necessarily have to be. For example: Upon returning to the class from a tour of Valley Forge, where General Washington had spent the Winter, each student will select some mode of representing his or her impressions, feelings, insights, or concerns. Some of the possible range of responses might be:

1. The construction of a diorama showing the geographical features of Valley Forge and its strategic military importance;
2. The building of model cabins where the soldiers were quartered;
3. The writing of stories, poems, or narrative accounts from hypothetical soldier diaries from that time;
4. The spontaneous "role playing" of the types of decisions made in the house where Washington stayed, or in the scene where Martha Washington joined her husband at Valley Forge;
5. The building of any game upon which the importance of the site at Valley Forge could be demonstrated, or any other expression or response by the student of the trip to Valley Forge and judged acceptable or better by at least 20 percent of the learners and the teacher.

This objective is open-ended in that any number of possible responses are acceptable. It is convergent to the extent that the zoo serves as the focus of the response. Rather than specify one response as the "right one," the objective specifies a broad range of responses which are appropriate and leaves to the judgment of the teacher its appropriateness. The objective is behavioral in the sense that it is within the range of responses emanating from a trip to Valley Forge from which learner behavior is to be judged. Eisner has called such objectives, "expressive." [59]

Prioritize Gap Statements

Once each educational objective has been checked against some measure or index of current performance, and a gap statement developed to spell out the difference, then the gaps must be clustered

[59] Elliot Eisner. "Instructional and Expressive Educational Objectives: Their Formulation and Use in Curriculum." *Instructional Objectives*. Chicago: Rand McNally & Company, 1969. pp. 1-31.

around the educational goals for which they are indicators of desired performance levels. Within each cluster the gap statements can be arranged by severity (difference between desired level of achievement or growth and the actual level). Across clusters the actual gap itself is not a good indicator of the severity of the need. Since the goals have already been ranked (and reranked) the curriculum developer knows which gaps are most critical to close by the place in which they were ranked. For example there may be a 65 percent gap in students recognizing Beethoven's Fifth Symphony, and a 23 percent gap in students being unable to read the editorial page of the *New York Times*. If the goal relating to basic skills was ranked higher than a goal calling for recognition and appreciation of great music, then the 23 percent gap must be addressed by the system and its resources first.

Publish List of Gap Statements

Once the gaps have been located by goal, a master list should be published without any hypotheses as to the causes of the "gaps," and without appearing defensive. The gaps should be explained and the process by which they were identified reiterated. At this point the needs assessment is done, but there are a number of critical and important *post* needs assessment steps which are recommended.

Post Needs Assessment Activities

Interpolate Gaps by Program and Level

To this point, the educational gaps or needs have not been part of a particular program. If there was a 23 percent gap in reading the editorial page of the *New York Times,* the gap was not placed in the primary reading program, the secondary English program, or the secondary journalism program. Rather the gap was identified outside of any curricular discipline or program.

Precluding at this time a restructuring of the curriculum upon which to locate the gaps for diagnostic review (which could occur as the result of examining similarities or dissimilarities in gaps) the curriculum developer will have to know who is now responsible for teaching the skills, knowledges, and attitudes and in what program. In other words, what program has the primary responsibility for teaching the required skills, knowledges, and attitudes? This means that the entire curriculum in each discipline must be laid out by grade level and the gaps matched to these statements as a matter of locating the problem area.

It will not be surprising that one of the reasons students are not learning a variety of specified skills, knowledges, and/or attitudes is that no one is teaching them. Gaps in learner performance are the result of gaps in teaching or in the actual school curriculum itself. Once a junior high school English department called in one of the authors and wanted to know what they could do about a gap in student skill with punctuation. The department had been involved in a local school needs assessment. They had ranked grammatical ability, *viz.* punctuation, as critical, along with parents and students. The school selected the Stanford Achievement Test subscales in language growth as germane to what they desired students to know. The results indicated that over half of the students had not acquired the ability to punctuate correctly.

When the teachers were asked why they thought students were not able to punctuate correctly, they replied that no one in the department really taught punctuation. There were a variety of reasons: it was boring to teach, the kids were not responsive, and few of the teachers were really trained in the approach required in the new English series. The department then went into a series of diagnostic planning sessions and attempted to close the gap in teaching and curricular emphasis as a result of being faced with a "gap" in student performance.

All gaps will not be so simply resolved. Some of the reasons for the lack of achievement in school are complex and interrelated with general societal or system problems. The interpolation step does not require an understanding of these causes, it is merely the step to locate the gaps by program and by level. The construction of a brief curriculum matrix with the subjects across the top and the grades down the side with brief comments as to expected skills, knowledges, and attitudes will help to locate the gaps in the appropriate disciplines and grade levels, or by whatever other method the school or school system uses to represent what is supposed to be learned in the school or school system.

Conduct Diagnostic/Planning Sessions

Gaps in student performance have now been identified in the current curricular programs and placed by grade levels. The needs assessment per se identifies the gaps—and the location. It will not specify why there is a gap. Once this has been completed, the actual needs assessment process is completed. However, unless the gaps become part of a meaningful attempt to improve learner performance, the assessment will largely have been a waste of effort and time.

Once the gaps are known, located, and prioritized, it is the responsibility of the curriculum developer to get together those who are affected and those who have a responsibility for acting professionally upon the information. A diagnostic session should therefore include teachers, students, administrators, and anybody else who will be affected by a subsequent discussion and development of implementation strategies.

Each facet of the educational program should be examined, such as:

1. Are teachers trained appropriately to implement the current curriculum?
2. Is enough time being devoted to the subject?
3. Are there unique characteristics of the student population which preclude the curriculum from being meaningful or appropriate?
4. Should the curriculum be rewritten, reconceptualized, or otherwise altered?
5. Are there adequate materials and supplies?
6. Are the teacher/pupil learning environments maximally productive? Are teachers overloaded? underloaded?
7. Does the current staffing pattern actually bring the expertise to bear which is necessary to solve the problem?
8. Are the testing instruments adequate measures to indicate the gaps?
9. Is the present curriculum adequate? well defined? validated? Does it match the objectives?

As these questions are raised, the curriculum group attempts to find causative reasons for the existence of the gaps. Probably no one reason alone will account for the gap or presence of the gaps. The group will have to test its reasons and its thinking on each of the hypothesized causes and arrange them in order of significance or in combinations. A brainstorming session might be held about all the possible ways the causes might be met and the gaps closed. The thinking of the group should be checked by other people and groups and when the priorities appear to be reasonably accurate then each of the strategies to close the gaps should become part of the budget planning for the future.

Part of the diagnostic/planning session is mapping plans for implementation. At this point detailed planning should accompany the implementation of each of the strategies selected to close the gaps.

Budget for Implementation Strategies

Educators often ask at what point a needs assessment is linked to the budget. At such time as the implementation strategies are selected to close the gaps identified, each strategy can be costed and placed within the appropriate budget program. If it involves reading, then the reading program may indicate a percentage increase for books, or in-service training, or increased utilization of reading specialists, or the development of reading centers in the schools. As questions come to be raised about why certain budget categories have been increased, the percentage increase can be linked to each strategy.

Budget development is then a reflection of considered utilization of data as it relates to validated school district goals and objectives. Theoretically, it may cost three times as much to close a small gap in reading, as to close a large gap somewhere else, because a smaller gap on a high priority objective may be necessary due to the increasing levels of complexity and the interrelationship of the causative factors.

Using a needs assessment as a basis for budget development, it will have to be decided how much funding it will take to maintain programs which are now deemed to be effective, and how much can be removed from these programs to shore up ineffective programs or to replace them to close critical gaps in achievement levels desired.

There are few hard and fast guidelines for such developmental activities. The fact that the budget building process assumes a degree of rationality that it did not have before makes it far less vulnerable to the political winds and to power groups with their own agendas who do not have the systemwide perspective required by the Board of Education. If a small and vocal group of parents is demanding that the Board increase its funds for musical instruments, and the available funds have been budgeted for the reading program, the Board is in a far more defensible posture to reply to the group: "When you were involved in the needs assessment you will recall that mastery in the basic skills was our first priority. We are taking the remaining funds we have and attempting to meet our obligations there first, while maintaining our music program at the current level. At such time as the needs (gaps) change due to varying values in the community, staff, and student body, and/or we are successful in closing the gaps in reading, we will redirect our funds to our second, third, and fourth program priorities."

Unless one actually deals with elected bodies, it may be hard to understand how they can be manipulated against the interests of the system as a whole without a defensible method for determining and defending the priorities of the system. No elected official can afford to be viewed as arbitrary and capricious. The public disclosure of the data in the needs assessment, the involvement of many constituencies in its development, is one method for establishing a bulwark against such undue manipulation, though nothing is ever foolproof in a political sense.

Fund Strategies

Each strategy for closing a gap can be funded, or if new funds are not available or old ones redirected, the top priority strategies can be funded. The derivation of strategies for separate funding and management can lead a school system toward more flexible management subsystems. Often called "project management,"[60] the strategies can be envisioned as temporary systems designed to perform a series of one-time tasks with definite objectives which can be assessed. A different type of evaluation model can accompany such thrusts.[61]

Implement Strategies

After planning and funding the strategies may be set into motion. Such strategies may be implemented within on-going programs, or new programs may be developed to carry them into implementation. The decision as to whether or not old programs are used as implementation vehicles may depend upon such factors as the competence of the personnel involved, the image of the old program, and the rigidities and traditions which may hamper a new concept. For some gaps, a bold and fresh approach may be required; for others, some shoring up of an already viable program may be all that is necessary. The advantages to old programs with familiar labels is that resistance may be considerably less than if a new program is developed which threatens

[60] John M. Stewart. "Making Project Management Work." In: Lesley H. Browder, Jr. *Emerging Patterns of Administrative Accountability*. Berkeley, California: McCutchan Publishing Corporation, 1971. pp. 331-49.

[61] See: Malcolm Provus. *Discrepancy Analysis*. Berkeley, California: McCutchan Publishing Corporation, 1972.

everyone including the old program which formerly had the responsibility of working in the area in which gaps were discovered to be present.

Reassess Gaps Via Feedback

After a given period of time, probably at an agreed upon point of assessment, testing data, formative or summative, can be carried to the organizing centers for programs designed to close gaps within the school system. Formative data can be used to correct the program as it moves toward gap closure. Summative data can be used to assess the effectiveness of a given program. Has the gap been closed? Were the efforts partially successful? If the latter is the case, then several more diagnostic sessions should be held to reanalyze the configuration of the causative factors. The point of the feedback process if the target is distinguishable is that data have a definite purpose for self-correction of any given program. Data are not only necessary, they are vital to program evaluation and program correction. Gaps should be continually assessed. Evaluation should be on-going and strategic to program design, implementation, and determining if a certain program should be continued, altered, or phased out. Programs are means to ends. They are vehicles to achieve the desired outcomes of the social system. None should be considered permanent, particularly if that means they are not assessed with feedback information regarding their effectiveness. The healthy organization should continually be in the process of creating and improving program vehicles with feedback. Any specific configuration of a program, that is, people, materials, time, facilities should be relevant to its purposes.

Repeat Steps 10-14

The needs assessment cycle is a continuous process and it should be repeated in its entirety, at least steps 10-14 continually and steps 1-9 on a periodic basis. As a part of the feedback cycle and examining the effectiveness of various programs and relationship to their ability to meet identified needs, the steps would be repeated.

Summary

The needs assessment cycle is a series of empirical steps aimed at establishing two indices for the purpose of determining the differences between those indices so that programs may be shaped to bring reality closer to a set of validated and prioritized conditions.

The needs assessment will indicate that differences exist, but it will not explain why there are such differences. The latter will be determined from a diagnostic review of the gaps revealed in the needs assessment process.

Purposive program planning as well as curriculum development can be meaningfully shaped from a needs assessment. Curriculum as a means to an end will depend upon such assessment as its ultimate purpose and the principal method for determining its adequacy and effectiveness. If the needs assessment process is bypassed, then there is no comparable method for determining the adequacy of curricula and/or programs on the basis of validated criteria. Inasmuch as the needs assessment cycle is a continuous process, curriculum as a means to an end is also a continuous process and must be constantly shaped and reshaped to maintain its relevancy, reliability, validity, and overarching purposes.

PART III

The Curriculum Development Cycle Using a Needs Assessment Base

A needs assessment provides the anchors of a bridge—the dimensions of (a) the current state of affairs and (b) the required state of affairs to which the curriculum bridge is to be built. It provides the rationale of the outcome gaps to which the curriculum is the "answer" to changing learner skills, knowledges, and attitudes.

The literature of recent years has been replete with discussions of behavioral (measurable, performance, etc.) objectives—some authors laud their importance, others flag their menace. It seems reasonable, however, that purposive design requires goals and objectives—and a needs assessment provides a relatively valid referent for setting goals and objectives for curriculum.

Many discussions note that objectives can be limiting, stifling, and dehumanizing since they only capture the trivial, the easy to note, the easy to measure. This can well be an important criticism of the effort which starts curriculum design with the mere exercise of setting measurable objectives. After all, measurability is not the equivalent of validity. On the other hand, a valid needs assessment provides a basis for setting objectives for curriculum which are based in reality—reality of the external world of people, and reality of individual differences of individual learners, educators, and community members. Curriculum which is derived from a valid needs assessment allows the creativity and contribution of professional educators to emerge and be harnessed in individually responsive instruction.[62] Diagram #2 indicates the "flow" of curriculum development when prefaced by a needs assessment such as described heretofore.

The starting place for curriculum development using a needs

---

[62] Kaufman, *Educational System Planning, op. cit.*

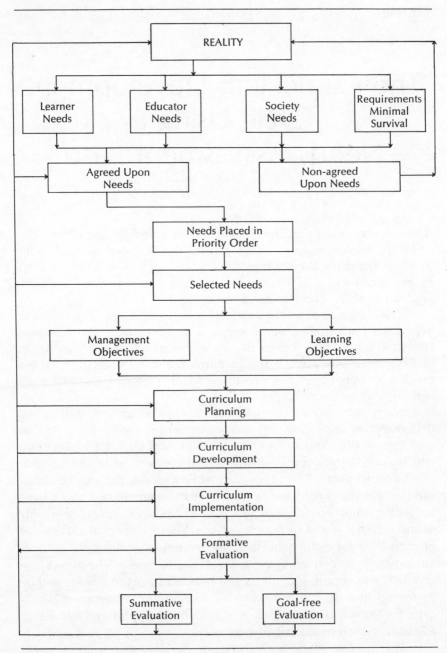

Diagram #2. The Curriculum Development Cycle Using a Needs
Assessment Base

assessment base is reality—the reality of individual learners, individual teachers and educators who support teachers, and community members in the environment in which they interact and live. This "reality" base is used to determine the needs (outcome gaps in skills, knowledges, and attitudes) of (a) learners, (b) educators, and (c) society as well as (d) requirements for survival, now and in the future in the external world.

These needs are "sorted" into two categories—needs which are agreed upon by the partners and those which are not agreed upon. The non-agreed upon needs are "cycled" back through the reality screen and the needs identification procedure of the partners. The agreed upon needs are then placed in priority order, and the needs of highest priority and criticality are selected for action. From the selected needs, management objectives are derived as well as objectives for learning.

From these management and learning objectives, curricula are planned, and then developed before implementation. During implementation of curriculum, there is a formative evaluation which can serve to "feed-back" performance information to any or all of the previous steps as required.

After the implementation and as many formative evaluation steps as deemed necessary, two types of evaluation are completed, a summative evaluation where objectives or accomplishment is assessed, and goal-free evaluation where unexpected results are assessed. Both types of data are used to refine and renew the system at any point in its previous development.

This curriculum development cycle thus forms a system which is self-correcting and self-correctable, and has the major features of what has been termed a "system approach" by Kaufman.[63] This cycle provides for a learner-centered and reality-based curriculum which will be individually responsive.

A System Approach

A process which starts with the assessment of the needs of the partners, relates the needs to survival and contribution in the world of work and world of relationships, puts the needs in priority order and selects the needs of highest priority for closure, develops and defines the most effective and efficient way of meeting the needs

[63] *Ibid.*

(curriculum) which implements and manages this curriculum, evaluates it during its use and at the end of learning, and uses the evaluation information to revise and renew the system is called a *system approach*.[64]

Responsive and responsible curriculum depends upon its being individually responsive to all of the learners—responsive in terms of their personal, emotional, and value characteristics, and in helping them to learn and grow so that they may be free, independent thinkers and citizens—not dependent upon others for their livelihood and their being. Individual responsiveness requires a formal assessment of needs, and relates these individual needs to the needs of all of the other partners—other learners, educators, and citizens, as well as the society as a whole (now and in the future).

Curriculum design which is thus responsive has been termed "IRI" by Kaufman, "Individually Responsive Instruction."[65] It differs from other similar sounding notions such as IPI (Individually Prescribed Instruction) in that the learner is a partner in determining not only how learning should take place but is also a partner in determining *what* should be learned as well. This differs from the providing of a relatively "authoritarian" prescription (such as a physician prescribing medicine for a sick patient) to learners by the teacher/educator. Individually Responsive Instruction (IRI) can best be derived from an individually responsive procedure of harvesting individual characteristics, desires, values, requirements and learning, and developmental, emotional, and survival needs, that is, from a needs assessment which formally dignifies each individual learner as a unique individual human being, and documents and formally lists these characteristics and requirements.

IRC (Individually Responsive Curriculum)

Individually Responsive Curriculum derives from such a formal assessment of needs, the blending of individuals with similar needs when such combination is sensible and sensitive, and goes forward from objectives which are based upon reality—the reality of the individual, the reality of the professional educator, and the reality of survival and contribution in the world of today and tomorrow.

A system approach is really a process for identifying problems and resolving problems. It includes a formal assessment of needs, and

---

[64] *Ibid.*
[65] *Ibid.*

makes such needs assessment a necessary and critical forerunner of curriculum planning and accomplishment.[66] A systems approach, on the other hand, is a very valuable tool for resolving problems, usually on the basis of the assumption of the needs assessment data and the resulting requirements. A system approach has the following steps, or functions:

1.0—Identify problem based upon needs

2.0—Determine solution requirements and identify solution alternatives

3.0—Select solution strategies (from among alternatives)

4.0—Implement selected strategies and tools

5.0—Determine performance effectiveness

6.0—Revise as required (at any or all previous steps).[67]

It might be seen that the steps and tools of needs assessment are related to the first system approach step (1.0—Identify problems based upon needs), and that curriculum design is related to the remaining steps, 2.0 through 6.0. Thus a system approach is a companion tool, or process, for assessing needs and developing individually responsive instruction (IRI) through individually responsive curriculum (IRC).

Other approaches to curriculum design might be viewed in light of the six step "system approach" process model to determine what parts of the total planning and doing effort of individually responsive curriculum are or are not included.

The system approach in general, and needs assessment in particular, are designed to define and deliver humane and holistic curriculum. It is humane in that it is individually responsive and includes each individual in the planning and doing of curriculum; it is holistic in that it attempts, initially and continuously, to be responsive to all of the characteristics of learning and learners, education and educators, communities and society. It attempts to both identify and resolve curriculum problems to achieve individual learning success.

Summary

A smash rock hit by Stevie Wonder, "You Haven't Done Nothin'," [68] prods us to remind ourselves that if education is to be really responsive, all partners must be included.

[66] *Ibid.*

[67] *Ibid.*

[68] Stevie Wonder. "You Haven't Done Nothin' " from *Fulfillingness' First Finale*. Stein and Van Stock, Inc. and Black Bull Music (ASCAP) 1974.

We have not involved those who are the recipients of educational services in their shaping, and needs assessment offers one formal approach for that involvement. If we want to hear the views of the partners, they must be asked, and those data must become an integral part of a holistic process.

PART IV

Critical Questions About the Needs Assessment Process

Many questions may come to mind about the ultimate effects of performing a needs assessment for a school district and using it as a basis for developing the curriculum and shaping the school system itself.

Will the commitment of a school system to needs assessment actually ruin system flexibility?

Some of the most asked questions about performing a needs assessment revolve around the fear of rigidifying the school system, paralyzing it as it were from becoming responsive to quick changes in the environment since it ostensibly has set itself on a pattern of determining its needs through a logical and orderly series of steps as outlined.

This is simply not the case. In fact, the opposite can be argued. A system without concrete and identifiable objectives is going nowhere. It can be pushed about from this force or from that force, but it only reacts. Such systems are "adrift," in the sense that they float above the confusion and are occasionally reactive to intense pressures. Such systems are very rigid and unresponsive. Without using a data base and without capitalizing upon the steps of a needs assessment our school systems have become socially insensitive. Numerous articles decry the implacable bureaucracy of school systems, while calls for de-centralization, more public involvement, and mandated changes by legislatures convinced of the slack in changing schools are evidence that our systems, without using data for feedback and direction finding, are now adrift.

A social system with a clear sense of direction and purpose has a perspective that those without them do not. Perspective occurs when the leaders can envision where and how the institution can change and why some changes are more important than others. Public confidence in the schools is lagging, perhaps because the purposes and goals of the schools are unknown.

A needs assessment has many methods for altering direction based upon data feedback and it is capable of change to accommodate new information. System flexibility is not ruined with incorporation of the needs assessment process, it is enhanced. Furthermore with the installation of a public and known process of problem solving, the steps used to reach decisions can be traced. Such retracing enables the system to avoid making the same mistakes twice, or at least subsequent decisions will be closer to the target.

The needs assessment process is self-correcting and flexible. It will not ruin flexibility nor spontaneity, nor will curriculum developed from a needs assessment be viewed with the same type of permanency that curriculum apparently enjoys at the present. While there is a lot of talk about curriculum development being a continuous process, when millions of dollars are sunk into a national curriculum, the feedback cycle may be woefully weak. By tying curriculum development to needs assessment the impermanence of curriculum is reinforced.

Curriculum represents a written down set of decisions. These decisions reflect under what conditions or in what direction the teacher should be going to arrive at a desired set of conditions or learner response. A curriculum by definition defines the learning process and establishes directions; so does a school. A curriculum does not ruin spontaneity any more than a school does. People govern spontaneity and curriculum can be constructed to encourage spontaneity; and schools can be more spontaneous and humane places than they have been in the past. As a tool, needs assessment is a closed-loop process which can be used to define and lead to more humane curricula and more humane schools.[69]

Where do standards come from?

The question of standards often perplexes educators who fear the imposition of standards generally, and those which may lead to unduly restrictive ones specifically. It should be noted that if standardized tests are used to generate needs, then standards are implicit in the bell shaped curve and in whatever the norming procedures were that

[69] Fenwick W. English. "Can Spontaneity Serve as a Curriculum Base?" *Educational Technology* 12(1): 59-60; January 1972.

were developed for that test. If no standards exist for the schools, they are carried in the collective heads of the teachers, each with perhaps a different set of criteria upon which success or failure may be judged in his or her assignment. To fail to state what the standards are for growth in the schools is to have whatever standards are used in the day-to-day operation dominant. The confusion and resulting inertia establish standards by default not by design. The point is that standards now exist and are used in all school systems. Are they the ones we should have?

In establishing goals, standards of achievement are defined collectively by consensus and reflect the aspirations of the community, the staff, and the students. If a school system feels that all of its graduates, unless otherwise severely impaired, should know how to balance a checkbook, or vote, or hold gainful employment upon graduation, then the standards are established relative to the criterion set by those groups. If, however, a criterion states that 85 percent of all graduating seniors will be able to read the editorial page of the *New York Times,* then the school is saying publicly it will accept the fact that 15 percent of its graduates will not be able to do so, and the school will be judged to be successful on this criterion of reading or citizenship as it were. This is not different from other such standards. If, for example, we say the nation is fully employed, we do not mean that we do not have unemployment. A figure of 4 million unemployed is generally used as the yardstick for determining "full employment."

This may require some soul searching, and it may be hard for the public institution to admit that it cannot be all things to all people. Yet, if reasonable, we should be willing to admit that not everyone will go to college, or be a doctor or a lawyer. We need plumbers and electricians, busboys and taxi drivers. Perhaps not all of them can read the editorial page of the *New York Times* with 85 percent accuracy or comprehension, or have to for that matter.

Somehow there is the feeling that the establishment of standards is so arbitrary as to confound the formulation of any standards. Yet the fact remains that most of the standards we use in education are arbitrary and used for convenience. What is 100 IQ? What is below average? What is the fifth grade? What is a percentile? other than yardsticks which describe certain types of standards we use in the practice of education. Lessinger estimates that at least one of every four students in the public schools fails.[70] Surely we can improve upon

[70] Leon M. Lessinger. *Every Kid a Winner.* Chicago: Science Research Associates, 1970.

this ratio, even while recognizing that as an institution we are not perfect and while there is much about our profession that is still mysterious and unknown.

Standards therefore serve as a focus for attainment to improve educational practice. They serve as benchmarks by which performance can be assessed, on the short term or on the long haul. Perhaps the function of standards is to remind us we have a long way to go and that our reach should always exceed our grasp. We are not less professional because we have standards and because our aspirations remind us of the distance.

As standards serve a useful purpose, so when such purposes are not served, they may be changed. If a given community will not accept less than a 5 percent failure rate to learn a specific skill and if the best efforts of the professional staff still result in 15 percent failure, then the 10 percent gap can serve as a basis for determining the next set of actions, from firing the superintendent to calling in a panel of experts.

If, indeed, we are dealing with some highly gray curricular and instructional areas, the public may come to value the purpose and function of educational research to a much greater extent than they appear to do now. Medical research is prized because doctors cannot yet absolutely cure cancer. As long as educators are loath to admit weaknesses in current practices there seems to be little push for research to find answers.

Will needs assessment result in the installation of more bureaucracy?

The minute a system is proposed which purports to establish greater system dependence upon school performance, the spectre of more bureaucracy is raised as one possible outcome. We have hinted that this is not necessarily the case. It depends upon the type of management models used by school systems as they attempt to organize the district to close the identified gaps. If temporary managerial systems are utilized the school system can avoid adding onto the bureaucracy and may even create a counterforce to further bureaucratization itself.

If, however, the management of the school system responds to the call for the support systems to perform a needs assessment and then act upon the data, there is no guarantee that more offices at the central or school level may not be the result. We simply say it is not inevitable.

Will needs assessment create a punitive environment for teachers and administrators?

The establishing of objectives, the gathering of data, and the installation of programs to act upon the data will not necessarily result in a punitive climate for professionals to work, unless one already exists. It is true that many school districts appear to be preoccupied with control and appear to be looking for someone to blame for a myriad of problems. A system which is largely punitive in its orientation to problem solving will have a hard time getting needs assessment off the ground, or for that matter, very little else which calls for examination of results.

However, since needs assessment is not an innovation per se, it is not the process that may be threatening, it is what happens in the system after the gaps have been identified. Will some people lose their jobs? Will the specification of those gaps in programs result in some professionals being held up to public or professional ridicule?

These human problems after the needs assessment should be addressed in the "planning to plan" stage. It should be clear that no one will be subjected to ridicule or that a person's incompetence will not be established via the identification of gaps in areas of their responsibilities. The identification of gaps is not a case for neglect or for anything else. This may not be true after a reasonable period of time has passed and the gaps have not been closed. In this case the process of diagnosis itself may have to be scrutinized as a variable again before professionals may be challenged as to why the gaps have not been affected by new or upgraded programs. Since needs assessment is both the establishment of direction and a process for system self-correction, the system should not be blamed for attempting to become better. It will be the responsibility of the administration and those in charge of the needs assessment process to establish these parameters well before the concept is put into practice and to keep reiterating them over the time period of the assessment and post assessment activities.

Needs assessment will not create by itself a punitive environment. It is a tool and as such is neutral. The values of those employing needs assessment should be the area to which the questions are directly addressed and how those values are translated into a management operation.

Will not needs assessment dehumanize education?

By dehumanization we take it to mean that some human beings

are considered less than fully functioning, potent (in a psychological sense) homo sapiens. On the contrary, needs assessment will be expected to enable the system to become more humane by making it clear which practices and programs are more effective, humane means to humane ends. Many schools without employer-employee assessment of their current practices are dehumanized. A host of practices create animosities and hostility and give students the idea they are dumb, less capable, that is, less than fully human. Needs assessment can call to task these practices and help eliminate them. Needs assessment is a method for determining if the collective behavior of the institution is compatible with and producing the outcomes the institution says it desires.

Will needs assessment help produce more responsiveness by school systems to innovation?

We have said that while needs assessment itself is not an innovation, but a process for determining if innovation may be necessary, once program and curricular gaps have been identified, the requirement for innovation or change may become more obvious. Whether or not such changes are radical or conservative depends upon the nature of the gaps identified and the strategies adopted by groups engaging in diagnosis after the needs assessment has been completed. In reviewing the various types of incentives for innovation in the public schools, Pincus noted that "many of the innovations adopted by the schools are not innovations at all, but only fads, since there is little or no serious attempt to validate them in terms of productivity or effectiveness criteria, nor is there any market-like mechanism which automatically separates wheat from chaff." [71] One of the problems in establishing such criteria as Pincus underlines and we have reinforced is that ". . . in contradistinction to many other local public utilities, the aims of schooling are unclear, or at least there is no consensus about what priority should be given to the various aims." [72]

One of the purposes of the needs assessment process is to make clear via consensus the aims and purposes of schooling which reflect national, state, and local priorities and involve at least three basic constituencies in the process: professional staff, community, and students. With the establishment of such clear goals and objectives, followed by good diagnosis about program effectiveness and preliminary work on budget development in relating programs to objectives,

[71] Pincus, *op. cit.*, p. 119.
[72] *Ibid.*, p. 114.

the system can establish an "anti-fad" but positive method for dealing with innovation, and begin to shed some defensiveness about "keeping up with the school district next door" in terms of innovation. We think that needs assessment is about the best approach to becoming more positive about education and less defensive about it.

What is the current scope of activities with needs assessment?

Kaufman has worked with needs assessment activities at the state and national levels. The Elementary and Secondary Education Act, Title III, among other legislation, is in many states establishing needs assessment at the state level. Many local school districts have begun to establish the machinery to create goals and objectives, though many are likewise missing some of the most important steps, such as in the validation process. The great strength of the needs assessment procedure is that it taps the various constituencies in a systematic way and at the same time leads to better public and professional consensus about what the goals of education should be, and what programs are most effective in realizing those goals.

What is currently the weakest aspect of the needs assessment procedure?

The most complex and difficult step faced by most schools and school systems with the needs assessment procedure is that of sampling problems. Sampling can become a very expensive item in the budget. Large communities may have to be sampled by mail which can be quite expensive.[73] A mailing survey is not returned by some of the critical audiences concerned with schools who may have been traditionally silent about the schools' ineffectiveness. For example, school systems serving large segments of culturally disadvantaged peoples, people who use English as a second language, migrants, Indians, present a problem for involvement if the school system does not have the person to use in the face to face interviews with sections of the community who remain isolated from it.[74]

Another problem for sampling presents itself with students and teachers. We recommend that all the professional staff be involved in some ranking of goals and perhaps matching of objectives to goals as

[73] For an example of one large school system's work, see: Norwalk-La Mirada, Norwalk, California, which was computerized.

[74] For a thorough review of sampling theory and methods see: Leslie Kish. *Survey Sampling.* New York: John Wiley & Sons, Inc., 1965.

a second stage validation effort. Depending upon the length of the matching process and the size of the student population, the students can be randomly sampled by age, sex, race, and geographic location within the community.[75] The reason for the total involvement of the professional staff is that it will be the staff that is expected "to act upon" the data. If they feel the data are not truly indicative of the staff's feeling, or the sample is not large enough, they may reject "ownership" of the gaps which have later been identified. To avoid this, most school systems plan for the entire professional staff to participate.[76, 77]

What happens if a needs assessment is not done?

If some procedure like needs assessment is not adopted, a process that is empirical and public and open to inspection, challenge, and validation, and by which school and school system goals and objectives are defined and prioritized, we will continue to be plagued by problems. Some of these difficulties are: confusion of means and ends, uncertainties over which problems are most acute, an inability to defend administrative decisions regarding program priorities, and a susceptibility to adopt new things before we really know what they are designed to do and what they will do when applied. In an operational sense we will still remain unclear about whether old programs and old curricula are adequate and should stay relatively unchanged or be updated with modifications, or whether new programs and new curricula should be instituted in a sweeping reform.

What is the greatest promise of needs assessment?

The greatest promise of a needs assessment is the operational creation of a viable and functional partnership in the administration, operation, and ownership of the nation's public schools.

Robert Kaiser reported the following advantages of a needs assessment procedure over other procedures in assessing attitudes and opinions of the community regarding public education.

1. It allowed for the involvement of more school-community groups.

---

[75] An excellent student sample was used in Sarasota, Florida, by Rick O. Nations.

[76] See: Joseph A. Sarthory and John H. Vigneron. "Identifying and Prioritizing Goals in Local School Districts." Kansas State Department of Education. (Xeroxed.) 20 pp.

[77] Department of Education. "An Assessment of Educational Needs for Learners in Florida." Tallahassee, Florida: the Department, 1970. 158 pp.

2. Respondents had the opportunity to express both their levels of expectation and their understanding of current practice.
3. A wide variety of responses was possible, which allowed for more diversity of opinion and opportunity for analysis. This resulted in more positive direction for the administrator in using the findings of the survey to improve the educational program.[78]

Is this the only needs assessment procedure around?

Certainly not. There are more than a few, all with some strengths and some weaknesses. However, most models only provide for the ranking of goals and objectives by the various partners in education, and thus there is no place for the introduction of new goals and objectives and the deletion of old ones—no renewal. These ranking-type needs assessments do have the advantage of getting community members, learners, and educators together and are thus a giant step forward. However, it is suggested that curriculum and its consequences are far too important for partial measures, so we encourage the introduction of two unique elements into any needs assessment procedure a system might consider: (a) the use of an external referent for individual survival and societal contribution, and (b) the introduction of criteria for possible futures for the learners after they finish with their formal education.[79]

Why all of the fuss about means and ends—is not education a process to begin with?

Education is a process, but it is designed to yield some rather staggering outcomes or results. If we talk about only the means, and never identify and define valid ends, we are risking dehumanization and irrelevancy. By focusing first on the ends, and then selecting the best means, we are keeping our curriculum horse before the cart.[80, 81]

[78] Robert J. Kaiser. "An Assessment of Educational Needs." Unpublished doctoral dissertation, Teachers College, Columbia University, 1973. 402 pp.

[79] Roger A. Kaufman. "System Approaches to Education-Discussion and Attempted Integration." In: Philip K. Piele *et al. Social and Technological Change: Implications for Education.* Eugene, Oregon: ERIC/Center for the Advanced Study of Educational Administration, 1970. Part III.

[80] R. L. Sweigert, Jr. "Assessing Educational Needs to Achieve Relevancy." *Education,* SCI, No. 4, April-May, 1971.

[81] Roger A. Kaufman and Richard Harsh. "Determining Educational Needs—An Overview," California State Department of Education, Bureau of Elementary and Secondary Education, PLEDGE Conference, October 1969.

Glossary of Terms with Needs Assessment

The vocabulary of needs assessment and system planning carries with it a terminology that differs somewhat from other terms encountered in curriculum literature. The concepts identified are more precise in usage and refer to very specific definitions. For this reason, these concepts are defined below as used in the text.

Needs assessment—The formal process for identifying outcome gaps between current results and desired results, placing those "gaps" in priority order, and selecting the gaps of highest priority for closure. It is, then, an outcome gap analysis plus the placing of priorities among the needs.

Need—A gap in educational outcomes or results. It is the discrepancy between the current results (not procedures or processes) and the desired or required results.

Curriculum—The sum total of experiences, methods, procedures, people, and things which are used in changing learner behaviors. It includes a series of educational decisions which determine the goals, objectives, content, methodology, and scope of all educational activities relating to achieving validated learner growth and achievement, including skills, knowledge, and attitudes.

Validation—The process for determining and showing that the results which were intended did in fact occur. It can be both statistical and judgmental, but involves comparing intended results with obtained results based upon internal operations and external criteria.

Goal—An outcome intent which is measurable on a nominal or ordinal scale, that is, which is stated in terms of a label or intent, or the fact that an outcome will be less than, equal to, or greater than a given reference point.

Objective—An outcome intent which is measurable on an interval or ratio scale, that is, which gives the following information: upon completion of the intervention (teaching, etc.) there will be a statement of what behaviors (including skills, knowledge, and attitudes) will be displayed, who or what will display these behaviors, under what conditions will the behaviors be observed, and what criteria will be used to measure the success or failure of achieving the desired behaviors.

Strategy—The methods for achieving defined objectives (or goals) selected, ideally, on the basis of what alternative ways and means are available, and selecting that which will give the desired results with the least expenditure of time, money, and effort.

Methods-Means—The strategies and tools used to achieve goals and/or objectives.

Process—The means by which one attempts to meet goals or objectives—equivalent to methods-means.

Solution—The means by which one attempts to meet goals or objectives—equivalent to process and methods-means. A "how-to-do-it."

Product—An outcome or result. The result of applying a solution, process, or method-means.

ASCD Publications, Summer 1975

Yearbooks

Balance in the Curriculum (610-17274)	$5.00
Education for an Open Society (610-74012)	$8.00
Education for Peace: Focus on Mankind (610-17946)	$7.50
Evaluation as Feedback and Guide (610-17700)	$6.50
Freedom, Bureaucracy, & Schooling (610-17508)	$6.50
Individualizing Instruction (610-17264)	$4.00
Leadership for Improving Instruction (610-17454)	$4.00
Learning and Mental Health in the School (610-17674)	$5.00
Life Skills in School and Society (610-17786)	$5.50
New Insights and the Curriculum (610-17548)	$6.00
A New Look at Progressive Education (610-17812)	$8.00
Schools in Search of Meaning (610-75044)	$8.50
Perceiving, Behaving, Becoming: A New Focus for Education (610-17278)	$5.00
To Nurture Humaneness: Commitment for the '70's (610-17810)	$6.00

Books and Booklets

Action Learning: Student Community Service Projects (611-74018)	$2.50
Bases for World Understanding and Cooperation: Suggestions for Teaching the Young Child (611-17834)	$1.00
Better Than Rating (611-17298)	$2.00
Beyond Jencks: The Myth of Equal Schooling (611-17928)	$2.00
The Changing Curriculum: Mathematics (611-17724)	$2.00
Criteria for Theories of Instruction (611-17756)	$2.00
Curricular Concerns in a Revolutionary Era (611-17852)	$6.00
Curriculum Change: Direction and Process (611-17698)	$2.00
A Curriculum for Children (611-17790)	$3.00
Curriculum Materials 1974 (611-74014)	$2.00
Dare To Care / Dare To Act: Racism and Education (611-17850)	$2.00
Differentiated Staffing (611-17924)	$3.50
Discipline for Today's Children and Youth (611-17314)	$1.50
Early Childhood Education Today (611-17766)	$2.00
Educational Accountability: Beyond Behavioral Objectives (611-17856)	$2.50
Elementary School Mathematics: A Guide to Current Research (611-17752)	$2.75
Elementary School Science: A Guide to Current Research (611-17726)	$2.25
Elementary School Social Studies: A Guide to Current Research (611-17384)	$2.75
Eliminating Ethnic Bias in Instructional Materials: Comment and Bibliography (611-74020)	$3.25
Ethnic Modification of Curriculum (611-17832)	$1.00
Freeing Capacity To Learn (611-17322)	$2.00
Guidelines for Elementary Social Studies (611-17738)	$1.50
Human Variability and Learning (611-17332)	$2.00
The Humanities and the Curriculum (611-17708)	$2.00
Humanizing the Secondary School (611-17780)	$2.75
Impact of Decentralization on Curriculum: Selected Viewpoints (611-75050)	$3.75
Improving Educational Assessment & An Inventory of Measures of Affective Behavior (611-17804)	$4.50
Intellectual Development: Another Look (611-17618)	$1.75
International Dimension of Education (611-17816)	$2.25
Interpreting Language Arts Research for the Teacher (611-17846)	$4.00
Language and Meaning (611-17696)	$2.75
Learning More About Learning (611-17310)	$2.00
Linguistics and the Classroom Teacher (611-17720)	$2.75
A Man for Tomorrow's World (611-17838)	$2.25
Middle School in the Making (611-74024)	$5.00
Needs Assessment: A Focus for Curriculum Development (611-75048)	$4.00
New Dimensions in Learning (611-17336)	$2.00
Nurturing Individual Potential (611-17606)	$2.00
Observational Methods in the Classroom (611-17948)	$3.50
On Early Learning: The Modifiability of Human Potential (611-17842)	$2.00
Open Schools for Children (611-17916)	$3.75
Personalized Supervision (611-17680)	$1.75
Professional Supervision for Professional Teachers (611-75046)	$4.50
Removing Barriers to Humaneness in the High School (611-17848)	$2.50
Reschooling Society: A Conceptual Model (611-17950)	$2.00
The School of the Future—NOW (611-17920)	$3.75
Schools Become Accountable: A PACT Approach (611-74016)	$3.50
Social Studies Education Projects: An ASCD Index (611-17844)	$2.00
Social Studies for the Evolving Individual (611-17952)	$3.00
Strategy for Curriculum Change (611-17666)	$2.00
Student Unrest: Threat or Promise? (611-17818)	$2.75
Supervision: Emerging Profession (611-17796)	$5.00
Supervision in a New Key (611-17926)	$2.50
Supervision: Perspectives and Propositions (611-17732)	$2.00
The Supervisor: Agent for Change in Teaching (611-17702)	$3.25
The Supervisor's Role in Negotiation (611-17798)	$1.00
The Unstudied Curriculum: Its Impact on Children (611-17820)	$2.75
What Are the Sources of the Curriculum? (611-17522)	$1.50
Vitalizing the High School (611-74026)	$3.50
Child Growth Chart (611-17442) min. order 10 for	$2.00

Discounts on quantity orders of same title to single address: 10-49 copies, 10%; 50 or more copies, 15%. Make checks or money orders payable to ASCD. All orders must be prepaid except those on official purchase order forms. Shipping and handling charges will be added to billed purchase orders. **Please be sure to list the stock number of each publication, shown above in parentheses.**

Subscription to **Educational Leadership**—$8.00 a year. ASCD Membership dues: Regular (subscription and yearbook)—$20.00 a year; Comprehensive (includes subscription and yearbook plus other books and booklets distributed during period of the membership)—$30.00 a year.

Order from: **Association for Supervision and Curriculum Development
Suite 1100, 1701 K Street, N.W., Washington, D.C. 20006**